Amelia Earhart

written by **Joeming Dunn**
illustrated by **Ben Dunn**

visit us at
www.abdopublishing.com

Published by Magic Wagon, a division of the ABDO Publishing Group, 8000 West 78th Street, Edina, Minnesota 55439. Copyright © 2009 by Abdo Consulting Group, Inc. International copyrights reserved in all countries. All rights reserved. No part of this book may be reproduced in any form without written permission from the publisher.
Graphic Planet™ is a trademark and logo of Magic Wagon.

Printed in the United States.

Written by Joeming Dunn
Illustrated by Ben Dunn
Colored by Joseph Wight and Robert Bevard
Edited by Stephanie Hedlund and Rochelle Baltzer
Interior layout and design by Antarctic Press
Cover art by Rod Espinosa
Cover design by Neil Klinepier

Library of Congress Cataloging-in-Publication Data

Dunn, Joeming W.
    Amelia Earhart / written by Joeming Dunn ; illustrated by Ben Dunn.
        p. cm. -- (Bio-graphics)
    Includes bibliographical references and index.
    ISBN 978-1-60270-173-1
    1. Earhart, Amelia, 1897-1937--Juvenile literature. 2. Women air pilots--United States--Biography--Juvenile literature. 3. Air pilots--United States--Biography--Juvenile literature. I. Dunn, Ben, ill. II. Title.

TL540.E3D86 2008
629.13092--dc22
[B]   2007051498

TABLE of CONTENTS

Timeline..4

Chapter 1
Young Tomboy 6

Chapter 2
Learning to Fly................................10

Chapter 3
A Plane Called *Friendship*..................14

Chapter 4
A Solo Flight................................18

Chapter 5
More Records................................22

Chapter 6
Lost at Sea................................26

Further Reading................................30

Glossary......................................31

Web Sites....................................31

Index..32

Timeline

1897 - On July 24, Amelia Mary Earhart was born in Atchison, Kansas, to Edwin and Amy Otis Earhart.

1908 - Earhart saw her first airplane at the Iowa State Fair.

1915 - Earhart graduated from Hyde Park High School in Chicago, Illinois.

1918 - Earhart worked as a nurse's aide at Spadina Military Hospital in Toronto, Canada.

1920 - Earhart took her first airplane ride with Frank Hawks.

1921 - Earhart began taking flying lessons from Neta Snook, one of the few female pilots of the 1920s.

1922 - Earhart purchased her first airplane.

1929 - Earhart helped found the Ninety-Nines, an international organization of licensed women pilots.

1931 - Earhart married George Putnam on February 7.

1932 - Earhart made her first solo transatlantic flight from Newfoundland to Ireland.

1937 - Earhart attempted her flight around the world, but she never returned. It is believed that her plane crashed into the Pacific Ocean on July 2.

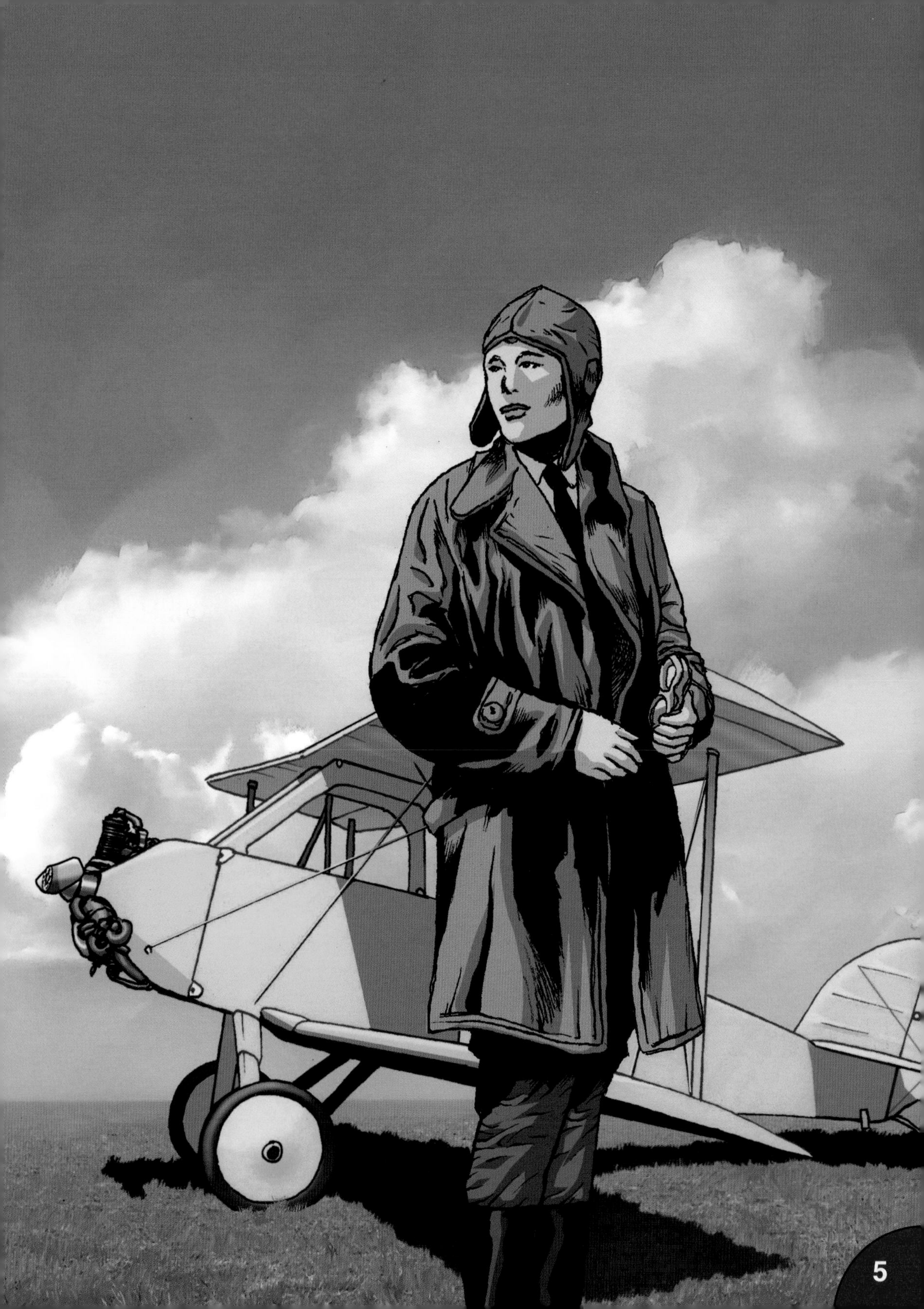

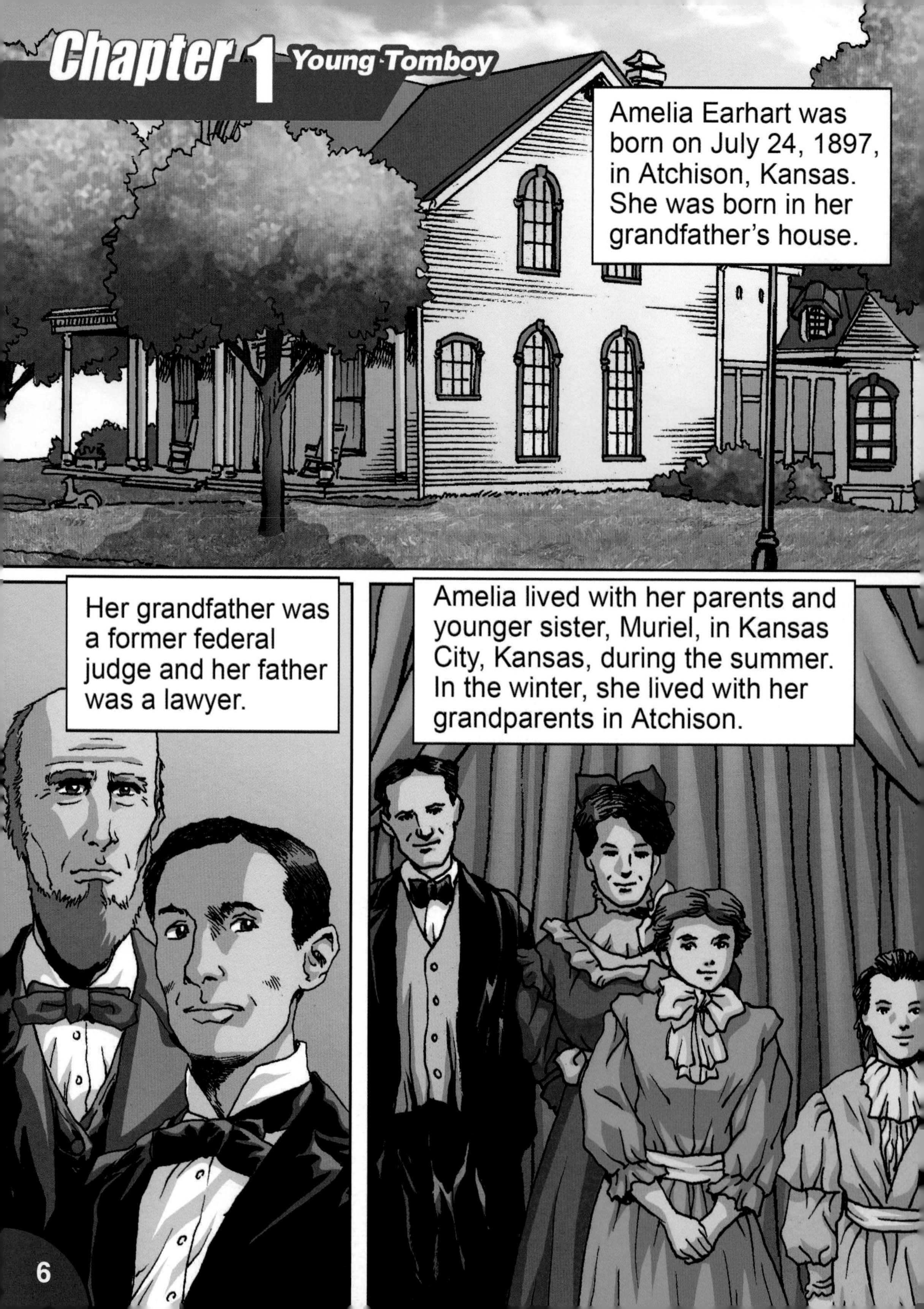
Chapter 1 Young Tomboy
Amelia Earhart was born on July 24, 1897, in Atchison, Kansas. She was born in her grandfather's house.
Her grandfather was a former federal judge and her father was a lawyer.
Amelia lived with her parents and younger sister, Muriel, in Kansas City, Kansas, during the summer. In the winter, she lived with her grandparents in Atchison.

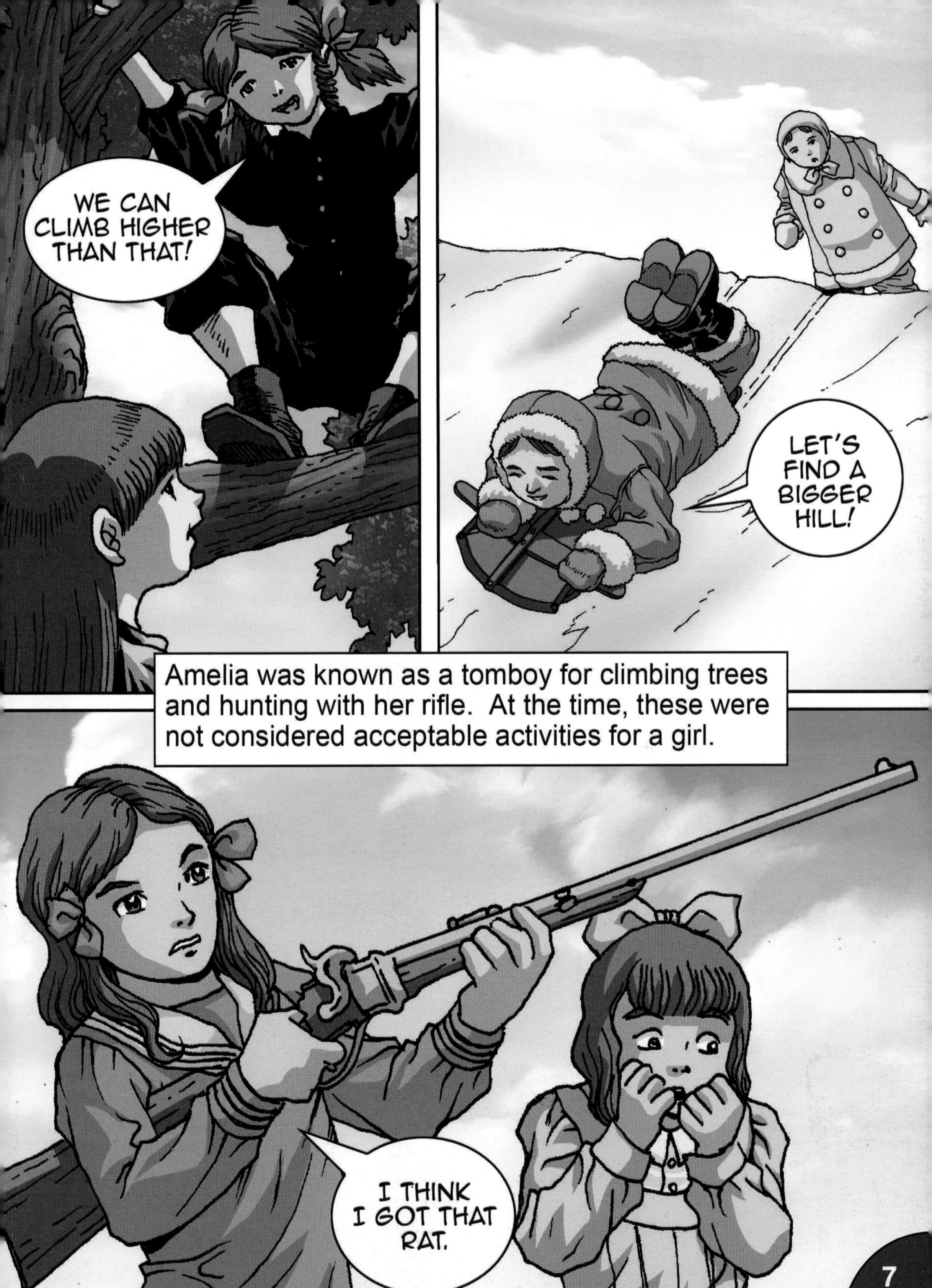
WE CAN CLIMB HIGHER THAN THAT!
LET'S FIND A BIGGER HILL!
Amelia was known as a tomboy for climbing trees and hunting with her rifle. At the time, these were not considered acceptable activities for a girl.
I THINK I GOT THAT RAT.

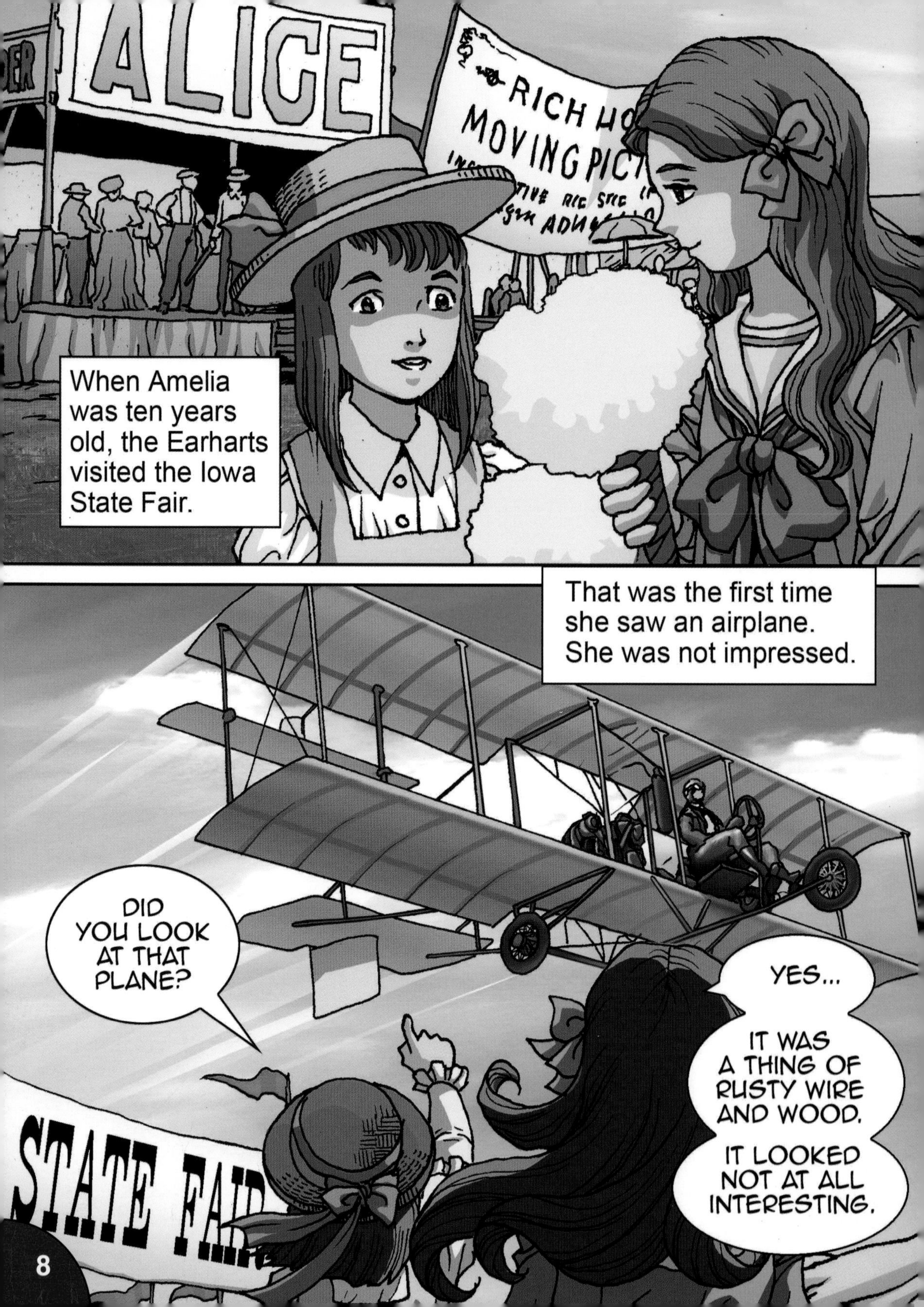
When Amelia was ten years old, the Earharts visited the Iowa State Fair.
That was the first time she saw an airplane. She was not impressed.
DID YOU LOOK AT THAT PLANE?
YES...
IT WAS A THING OF RUSTY WIRE AND WOOD.
IT LOOKED NOT AT ALL INTERESTING.

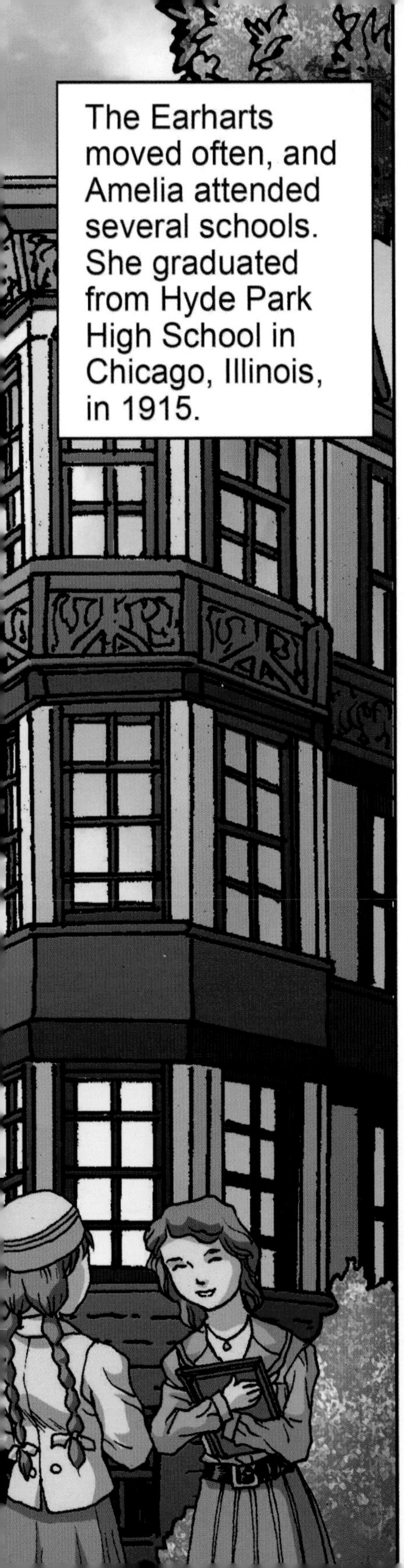
The Earharts moved often, and Amelia attended several schools. She graduated from Hyde Park High School in Chicago, Illinois, in 1915.

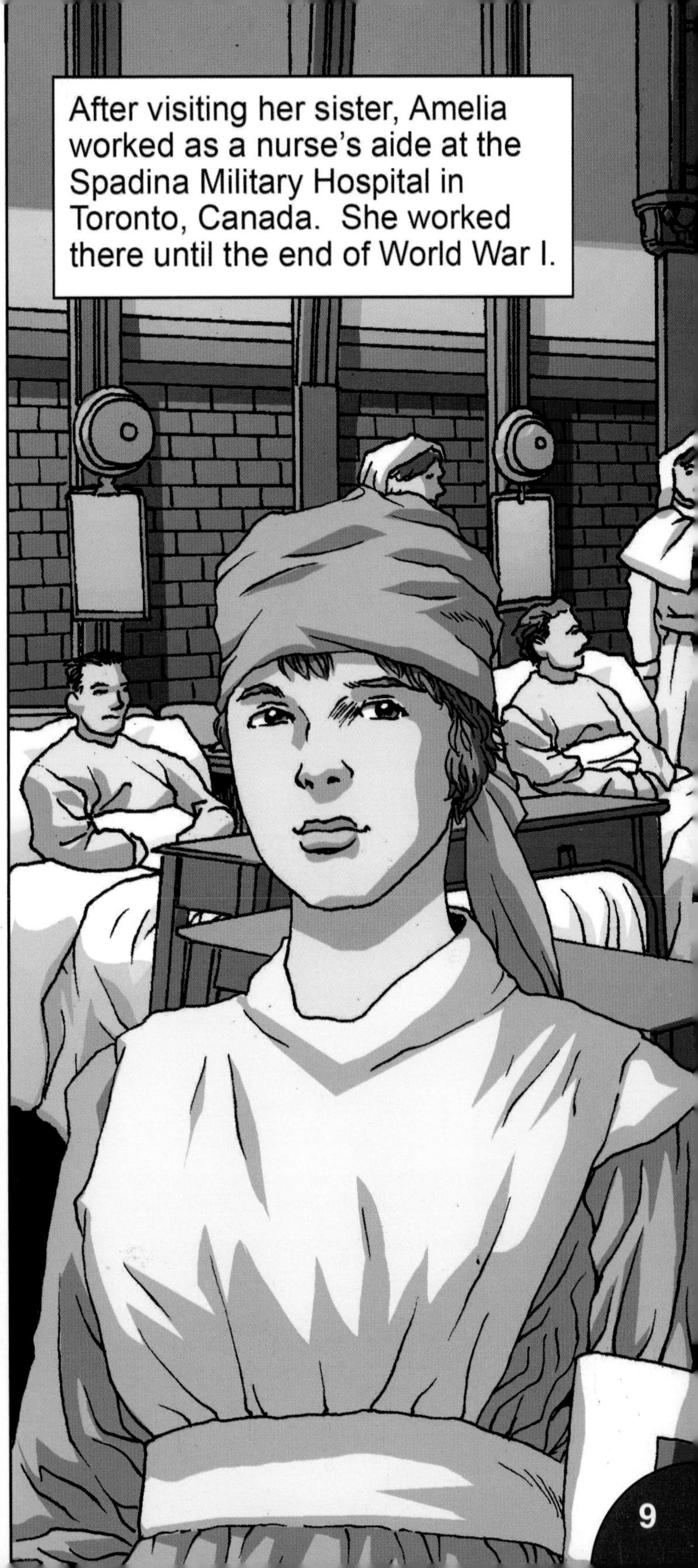
After visiting her sister, Amelia worked as a nurse's aide at the Spadina Military Hospital in Toronto, Canada. She worked there until the end of World War I.

Chapter 2 Learning to Fly

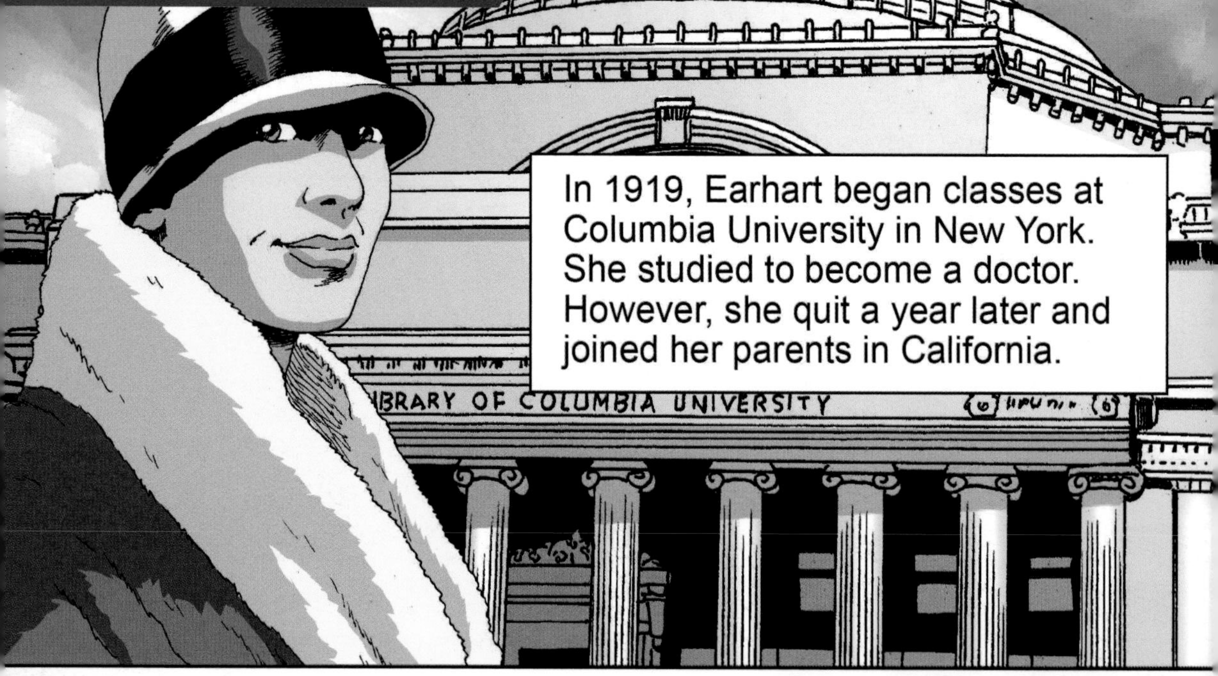
In 1919, Earhart began classes at Columbia University in New York. She studied to become a doctor. However, she quit a year later and joined her parents in California.
LIBRARY OF COLUMBIA UNIVERSITY

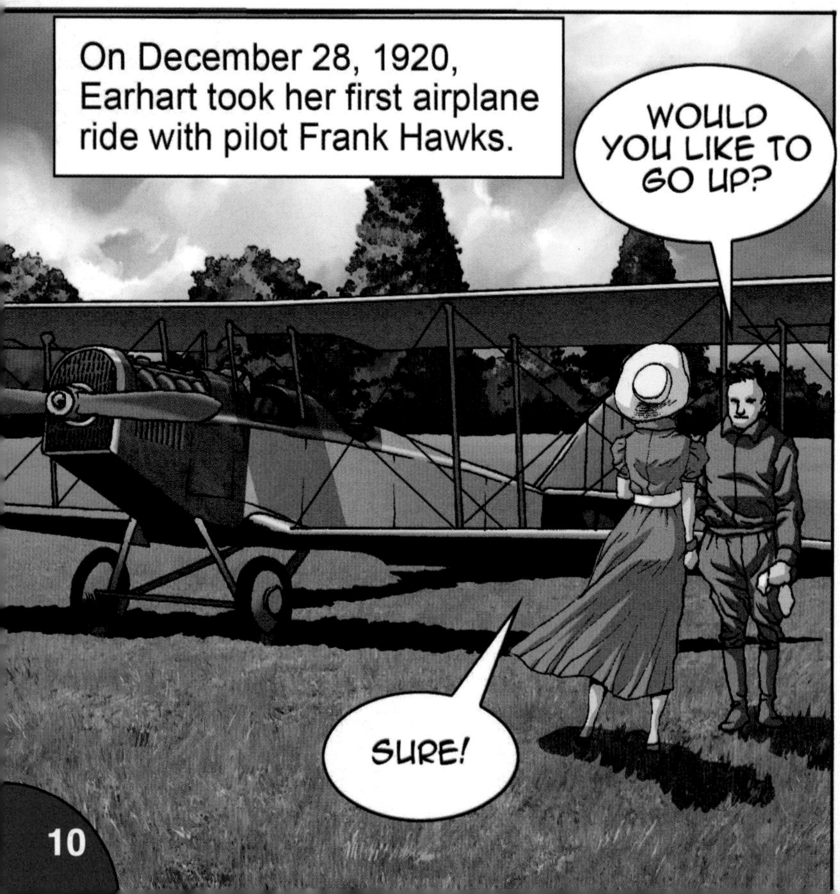
On December 28, 1920, Earhart took her first airplane ride with pilot Frank Hawks.
WOULD YOU LIKE TO GO UP?
SURE!

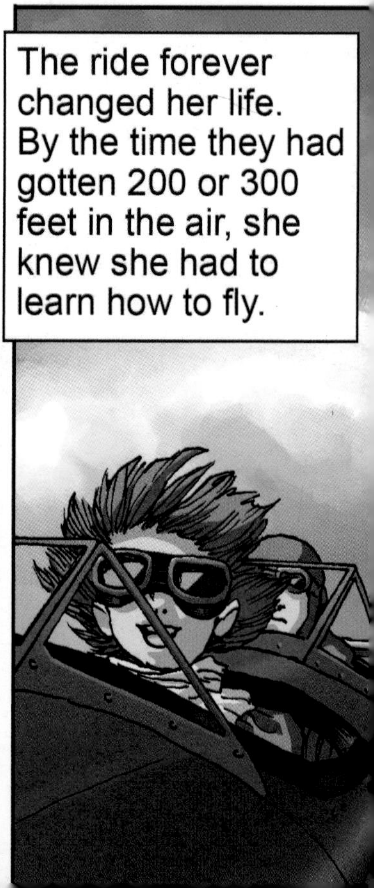
The ride forever changed her life. By the time they had gotten 200 or 300 feet in the air, she knew she had to learn how to fly.

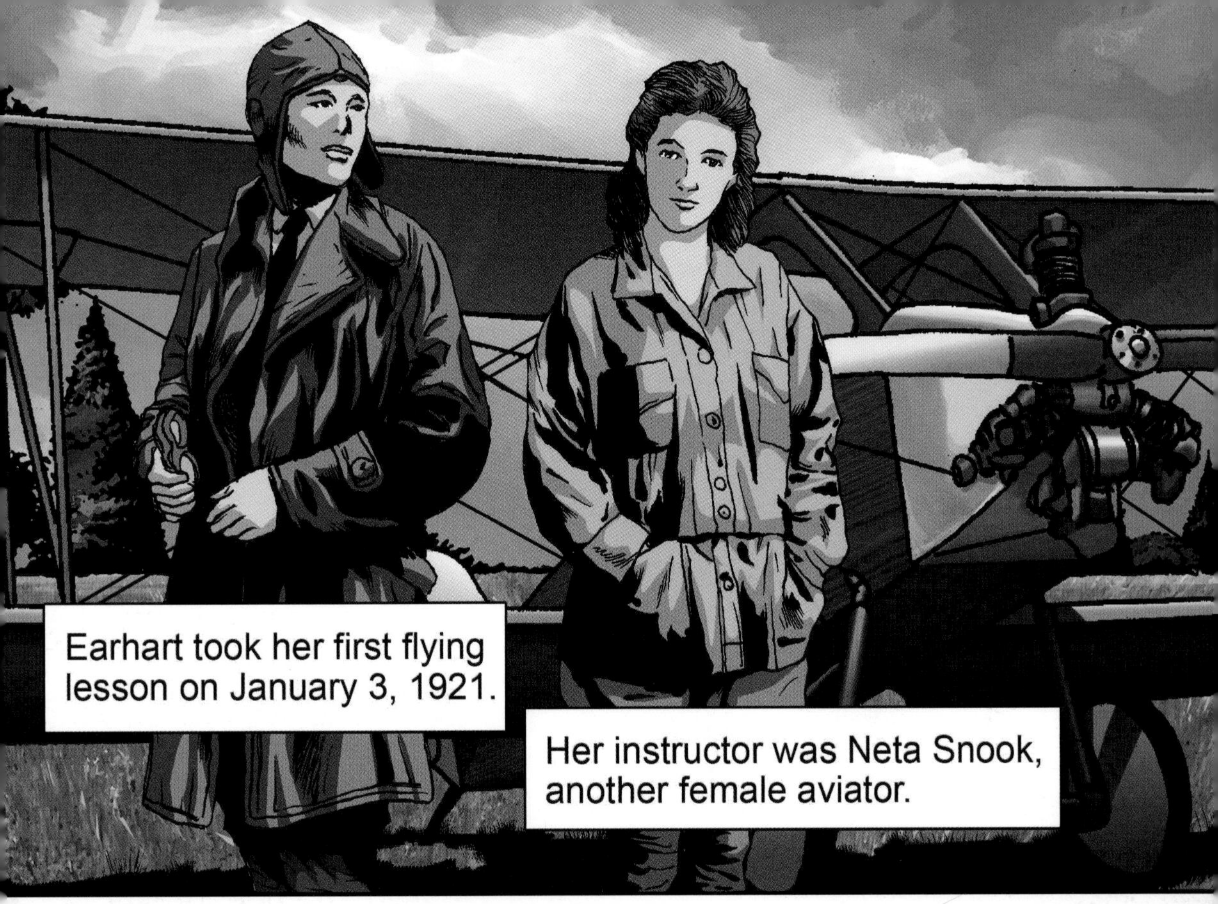

Earhart took her first flying lesson on January 3, 1921.
Her instructor was Neta Snook, another female aviator.

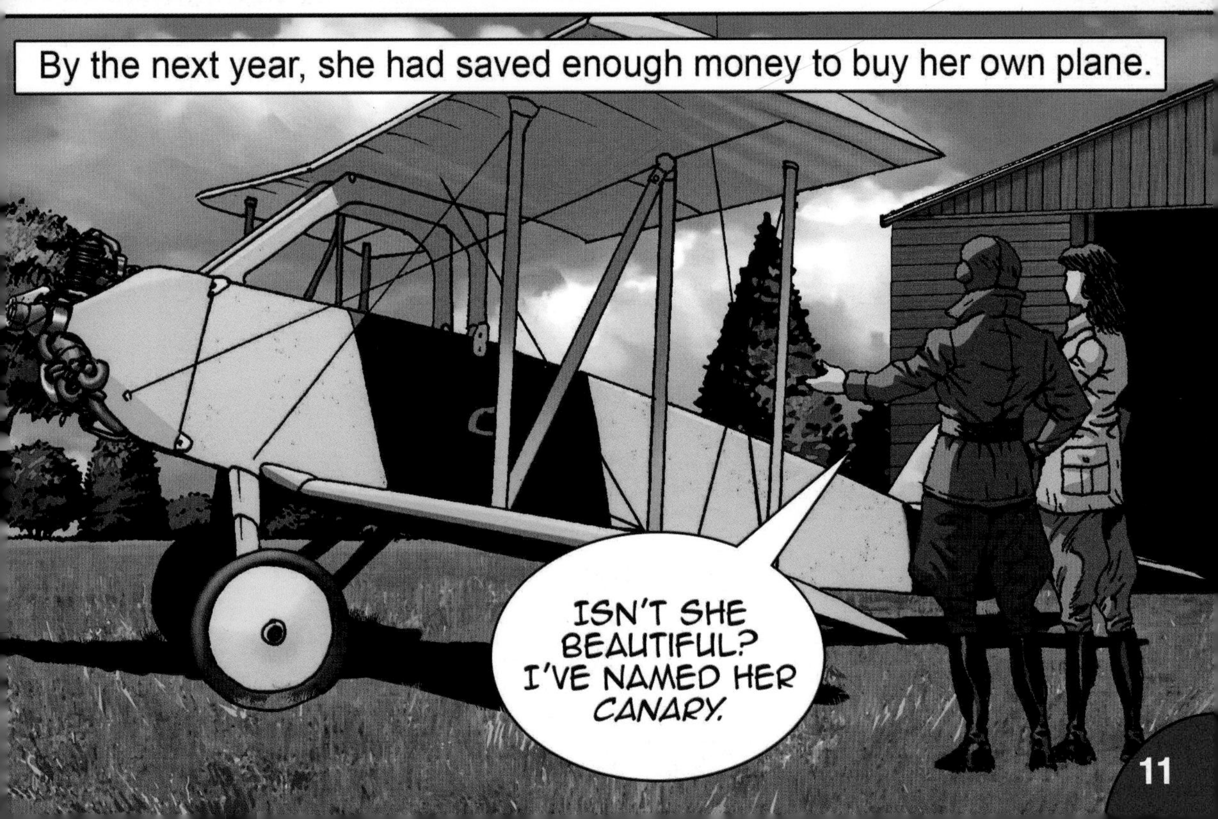

By the next year, she had saved enough money to buy her own plane.
ISN'T SHE BEAUTIFUL? I'VE NAMED HER *CANARY.*

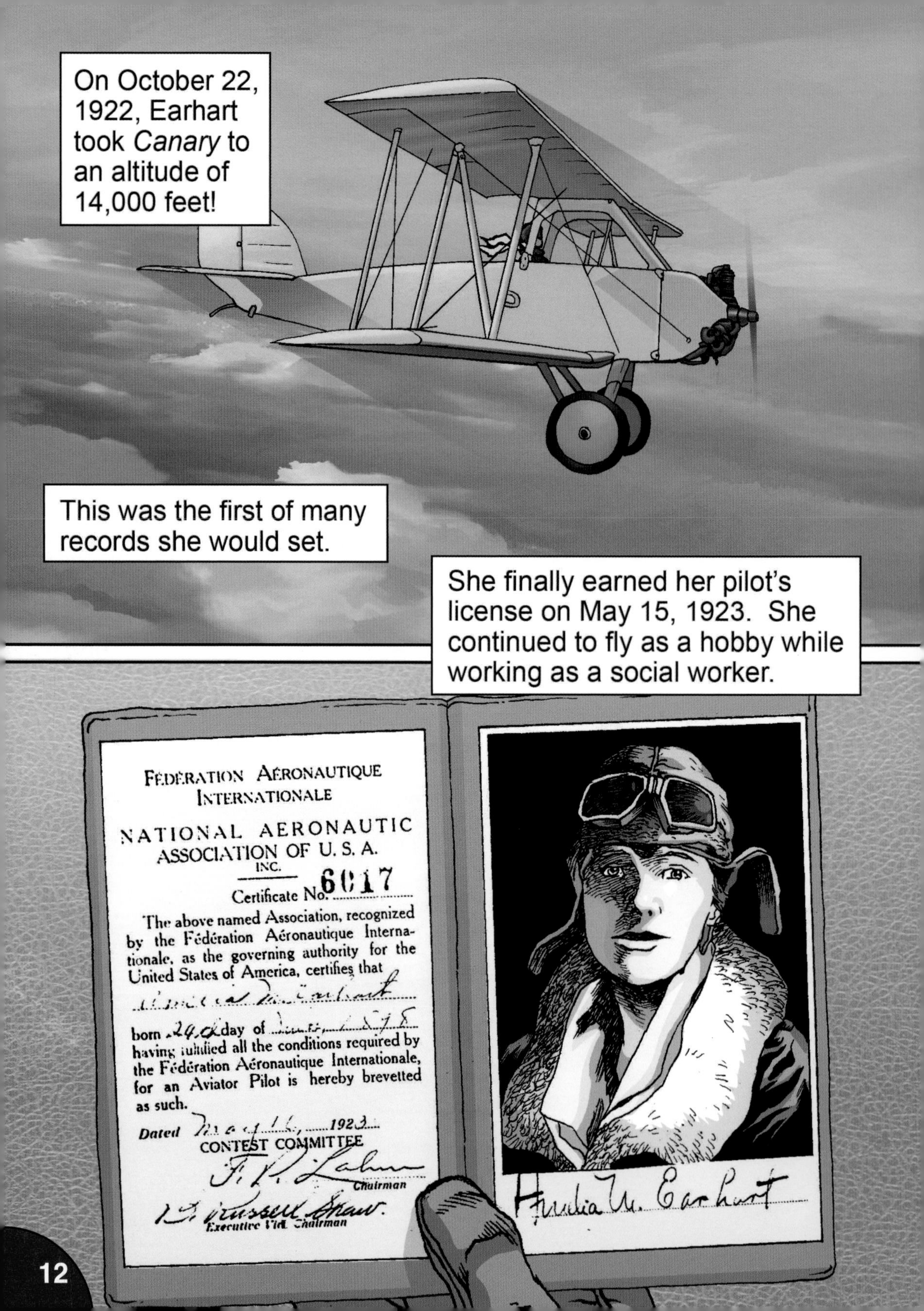
On October 22, 1922, Earhart took *Canary* to an altitude of 14,000 feet!
This was the first of many records she would set.
She finally earned her pilot's license on May 15, 1923. She continued to fly as a hobby while working as a social worker.
FÉDÉRATION AÉRONAUTIQUE INTERNATIONALE
NATIONAL AERONAUTIC ASSOCIATION OF U. S. A. INC.
Certificate No. 6017
The above named Association, recognized by the Fédération Aéronautique Internationale, as the governing authority for the United States of America, certifies that
born day of
having fulfilled all the conditions required by the Fédération Aéronautique Internationale, for an Aviator Pilot is hereby brevetted as such.
Dated 1923
CONTEST COMMITTEE
Chairman
Executive Vice Chairman

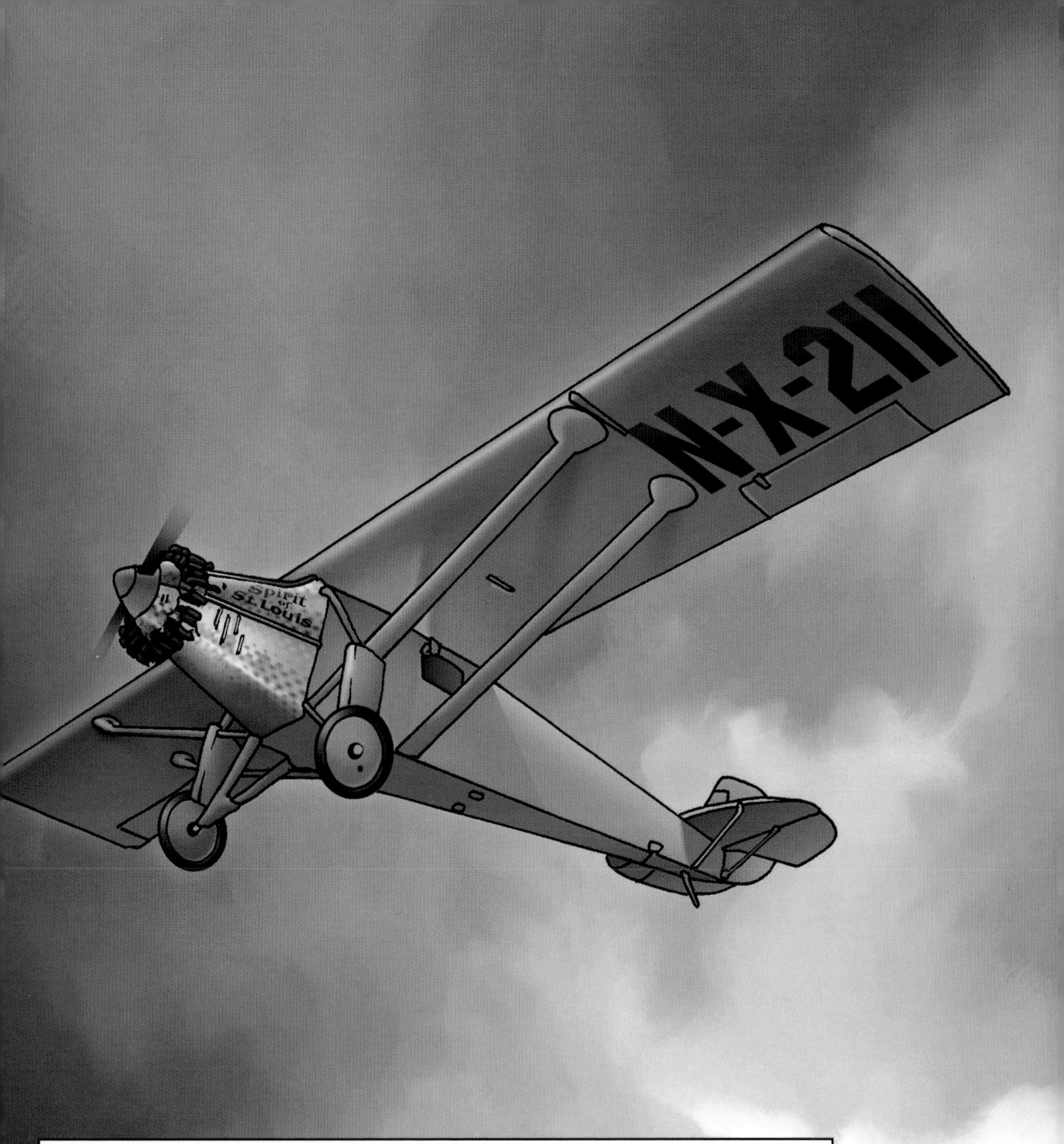
Spirit of St. Louis
N-X-211

On May 20, 1927, Charles Lindbergh flew solo across the Atlantic Ocean on the *Spirit of St. Louis*. He left Roosevelt Field in New York. Thirty-three and a half hours later, he landed in Paris, France. Interest in flying started to grow after this amazing flight.

Chapter 3 A Plane Called Friendship

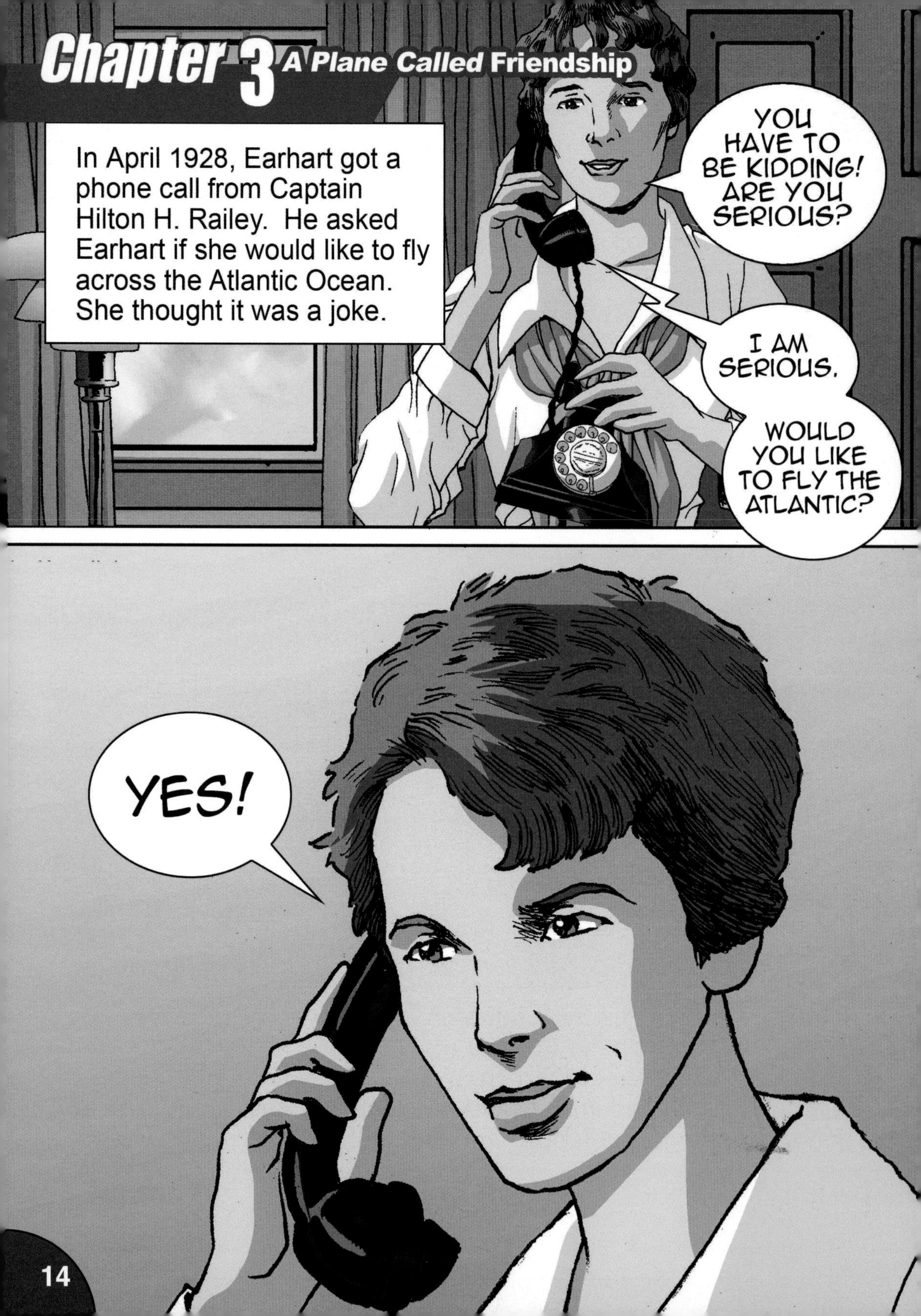

In April 1928, Earhart got a phone call from Captain Hilton H. Railey. He asked Earhart if she would like to fly across the Atlantic Ocean. She thought it was a joke.
YOU HAVE TO BE KIDDING! ARE YOU SERIOUS?
I AM SERIOUS.
WOULD YOU LIKE TO FLY THE ATLANTIC?
YES!

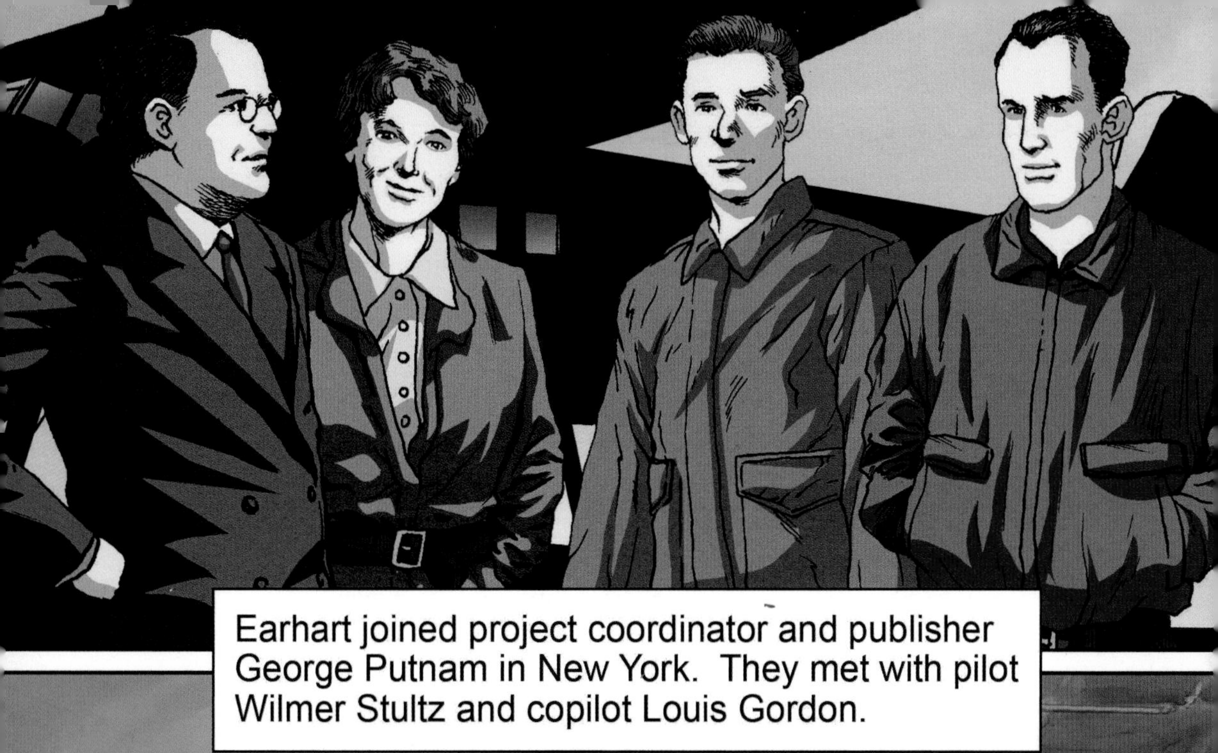
Earhart joined project coordinator and publisher George Putnam in New York. They met with pilot Wilmer Stultz and copilot Louis Gordon.

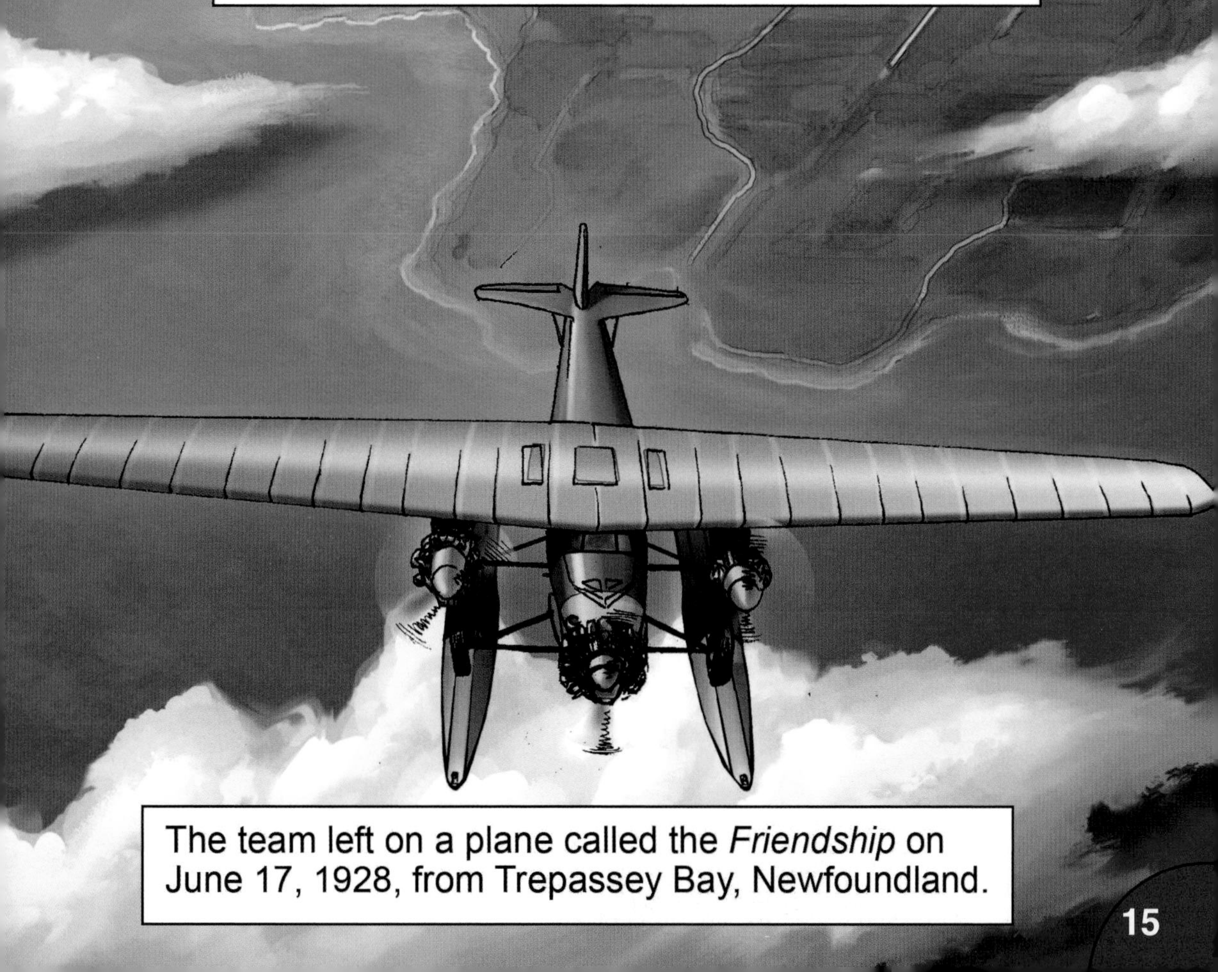
The team left on a plane called the *Friendship* on June 17, 1928, from Trepassey Bay, Newfoundland.

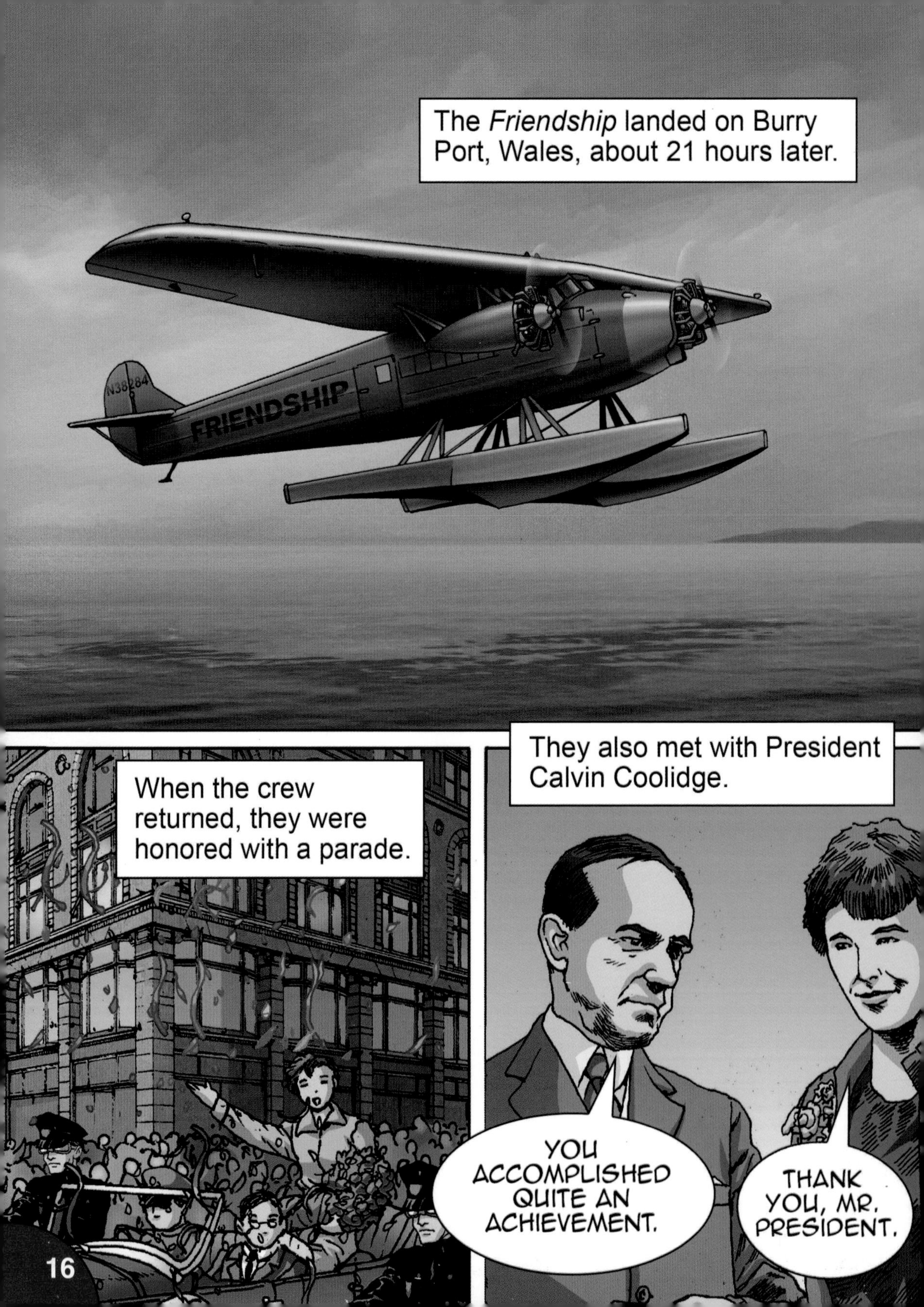
The *Friendship* landed on Burry Port, Wales, about 21 hours later.
FRIENDSHIP
N38284
When the crew returned, they were honored with a parade.
They also met with President Calvin Coolidge.
YOU ACCOMPLISHED QUITE AN ACHIEVEMENT.
THANK YOU, MR. PRESIDENT.

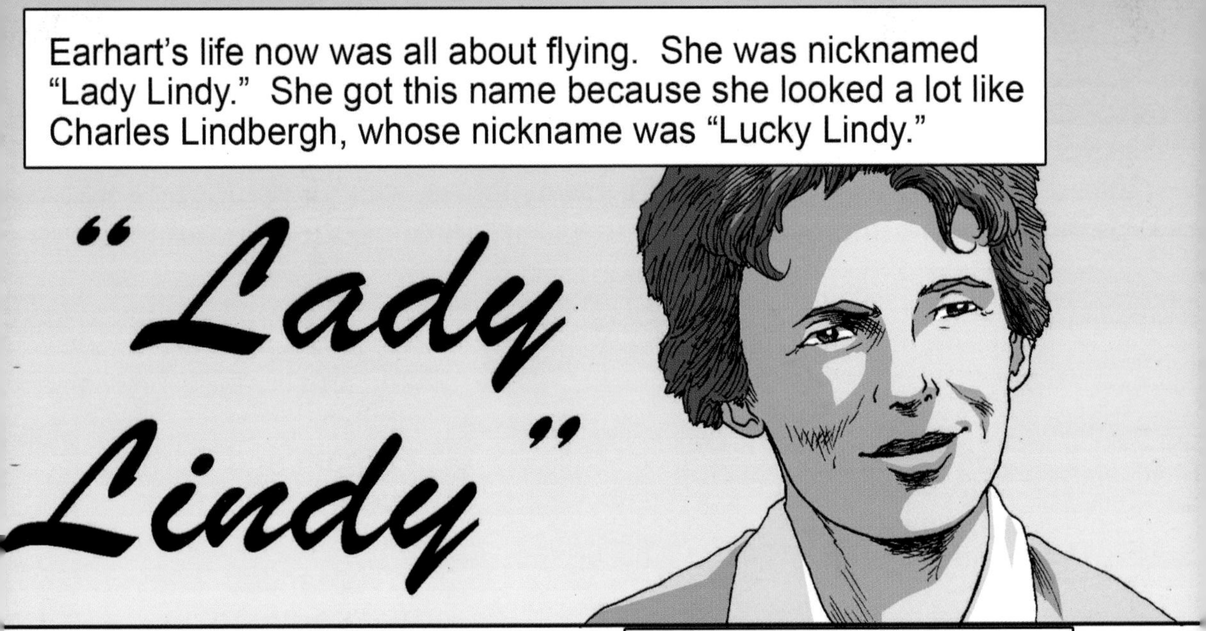
Earhart's life now was all about flying. She was nicknamed "Lady Lindy." She got this name because she looked a lot like Charles Lindbergh, whose nickname was "Lucky Lindy."
"Lady Lindy"

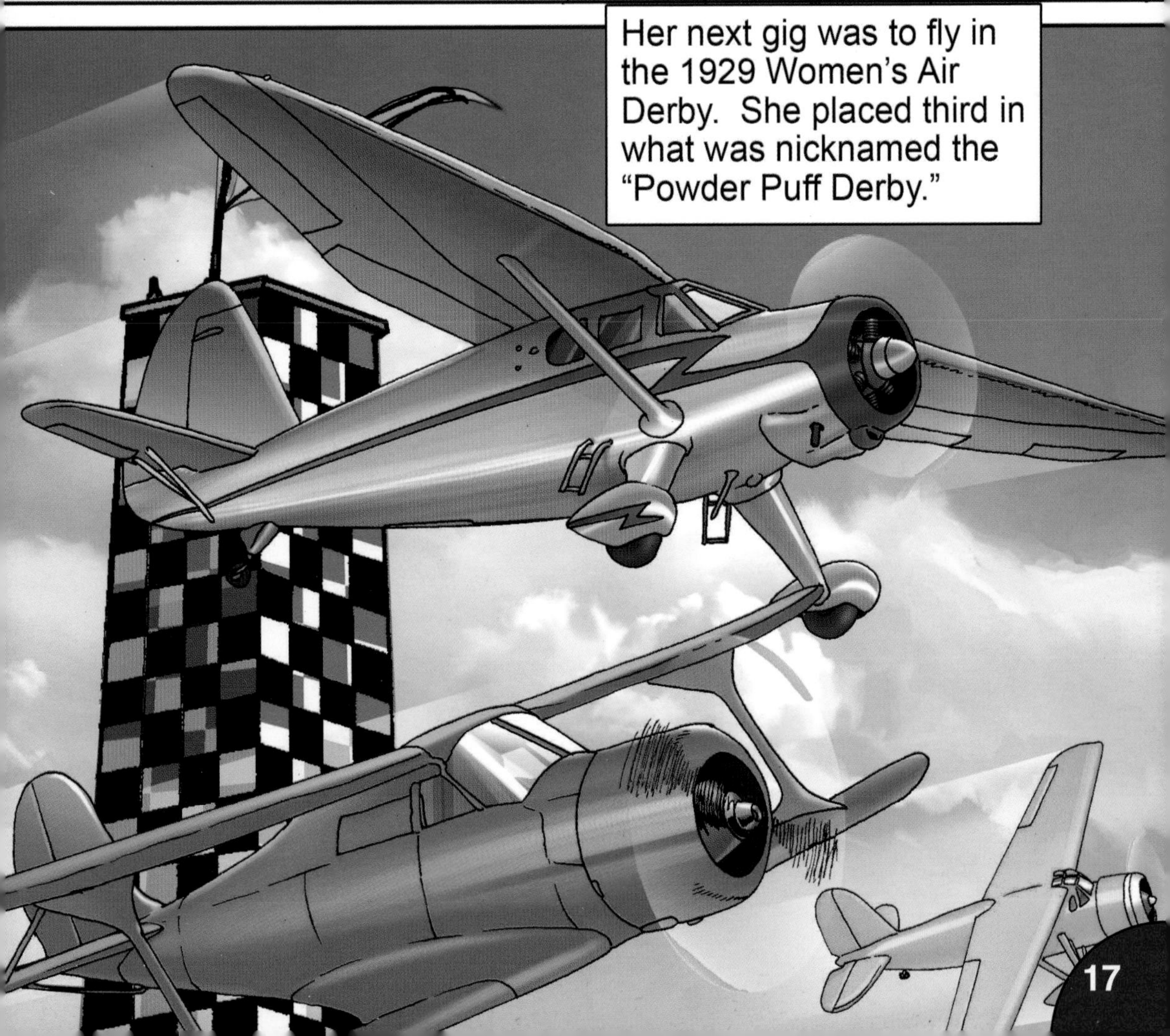
Her next gig was to fly in the 1929 Women's Air Derby. She placed third in what was nicknamed the "Powder Puff Derby."

Chapter 4 A Solo Flight

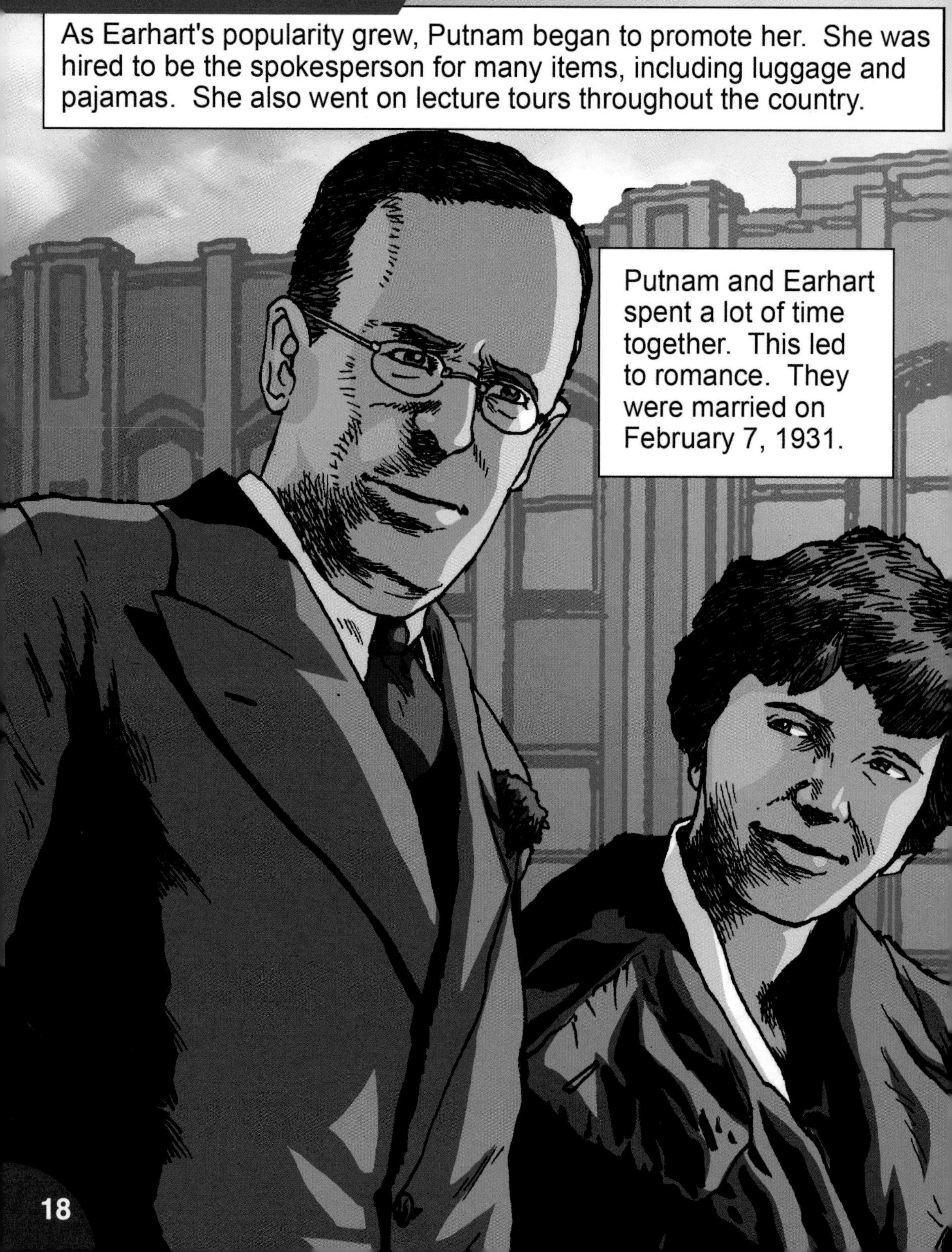
As Earhart's popularity grew, Putnam began to promote her. She was hired to be the spokesperson for many items, including luggage and pajamas. She also went on lecture tours throughout the country.
Putnam and Earhart spent a lot of time together. This led to romance. They were married on February 7, 1931.

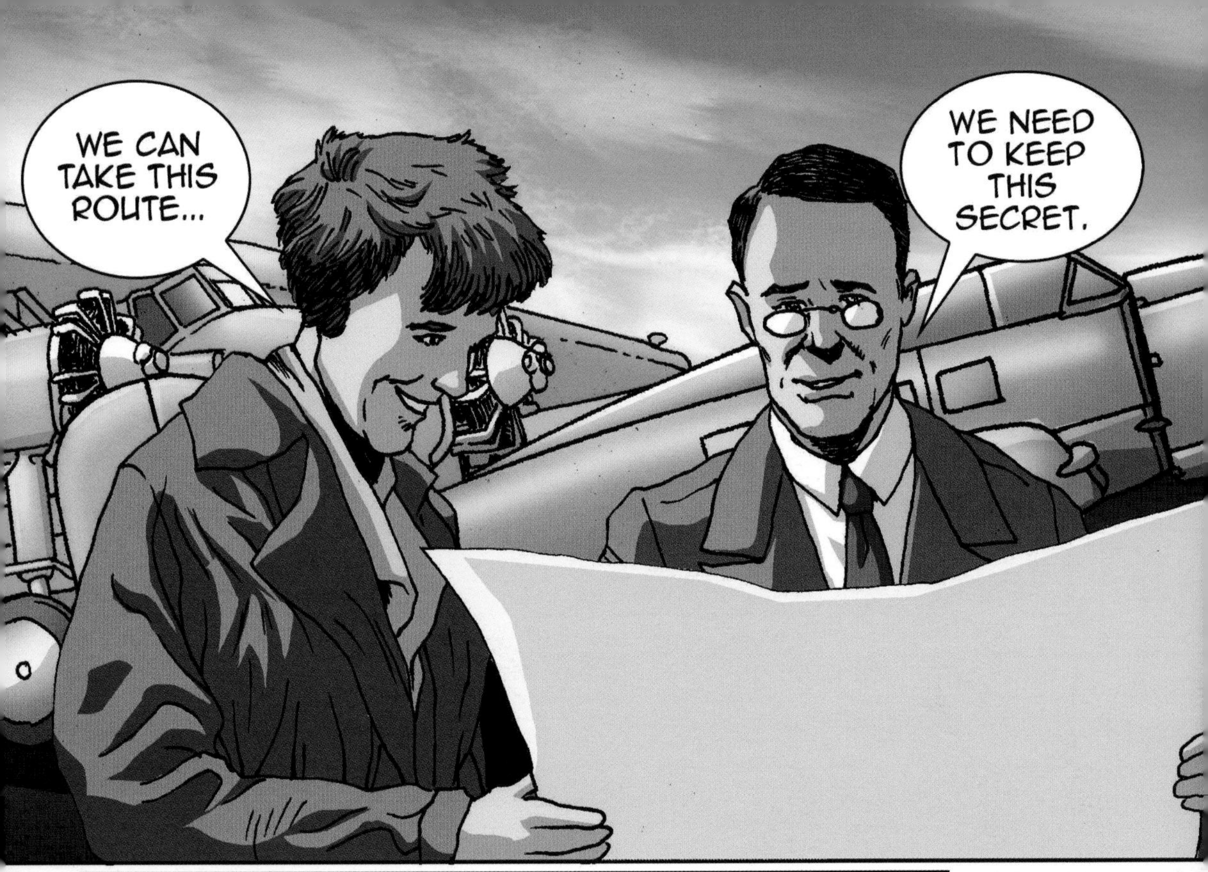
WE CAN TAKE THIS ROUTE...
WE NEED TO KEEP THIS SECRET.

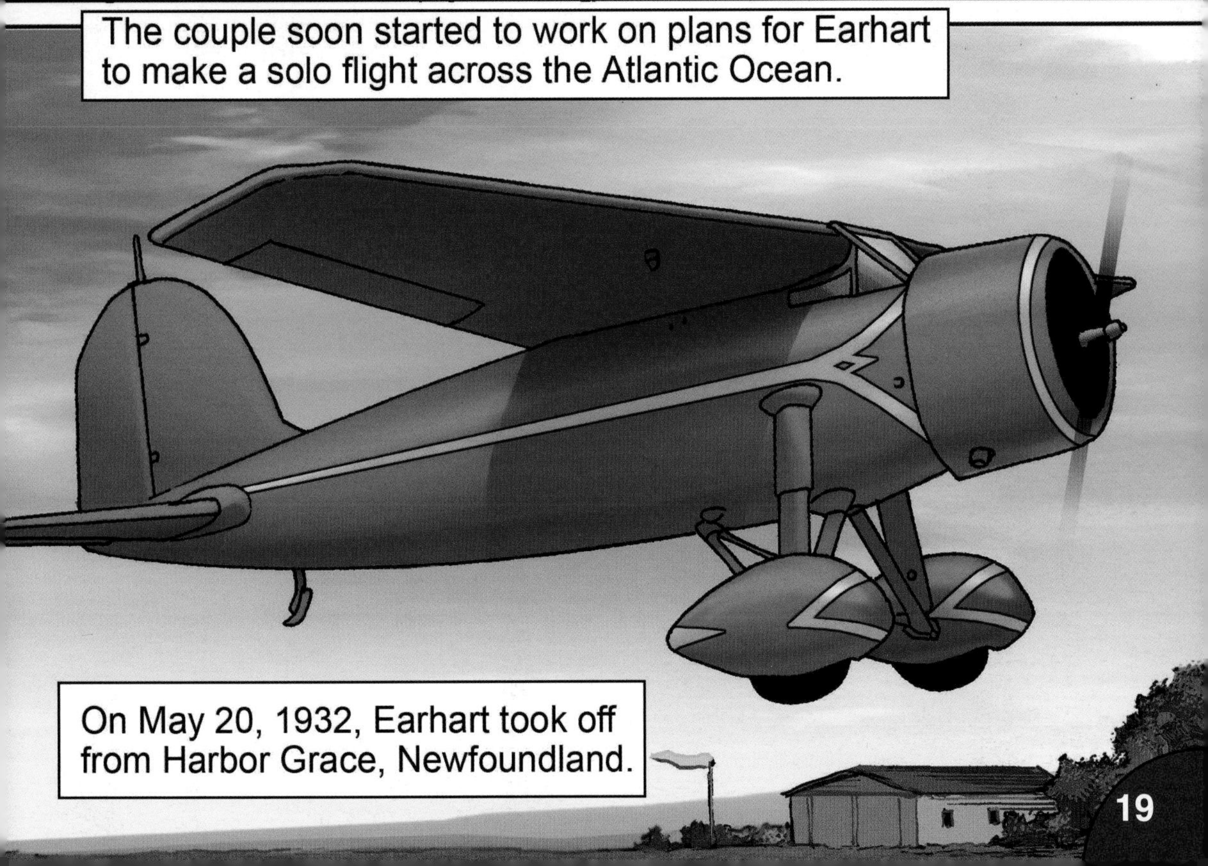
The couple soon started to work on plans for Earhart to make a solo flight across the Atlantic Ocean.
On May 20, 1932, Earhart took off from Harbor Grace, Newfoundland.

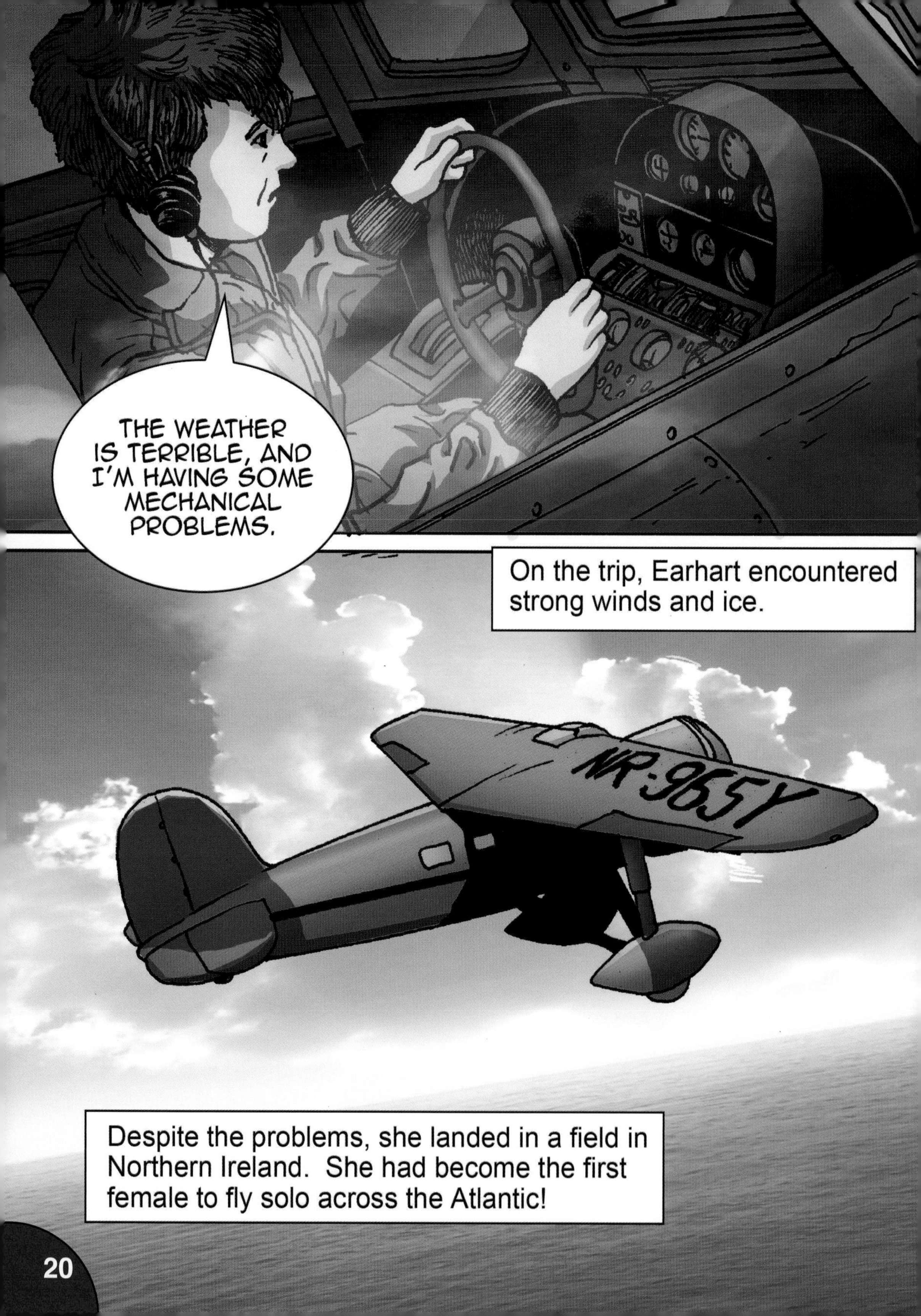
THE WEATHER IS TERRIBLE, AND I'M HAVING SOME MECHANICAL PROBLEMS.
On the trip, Earhart encountered strong winds and ice.
NR-965Y
Despite the problems, she landed in a field in Northern Ireland. She had become the first female to fly solo across the Atlantic!

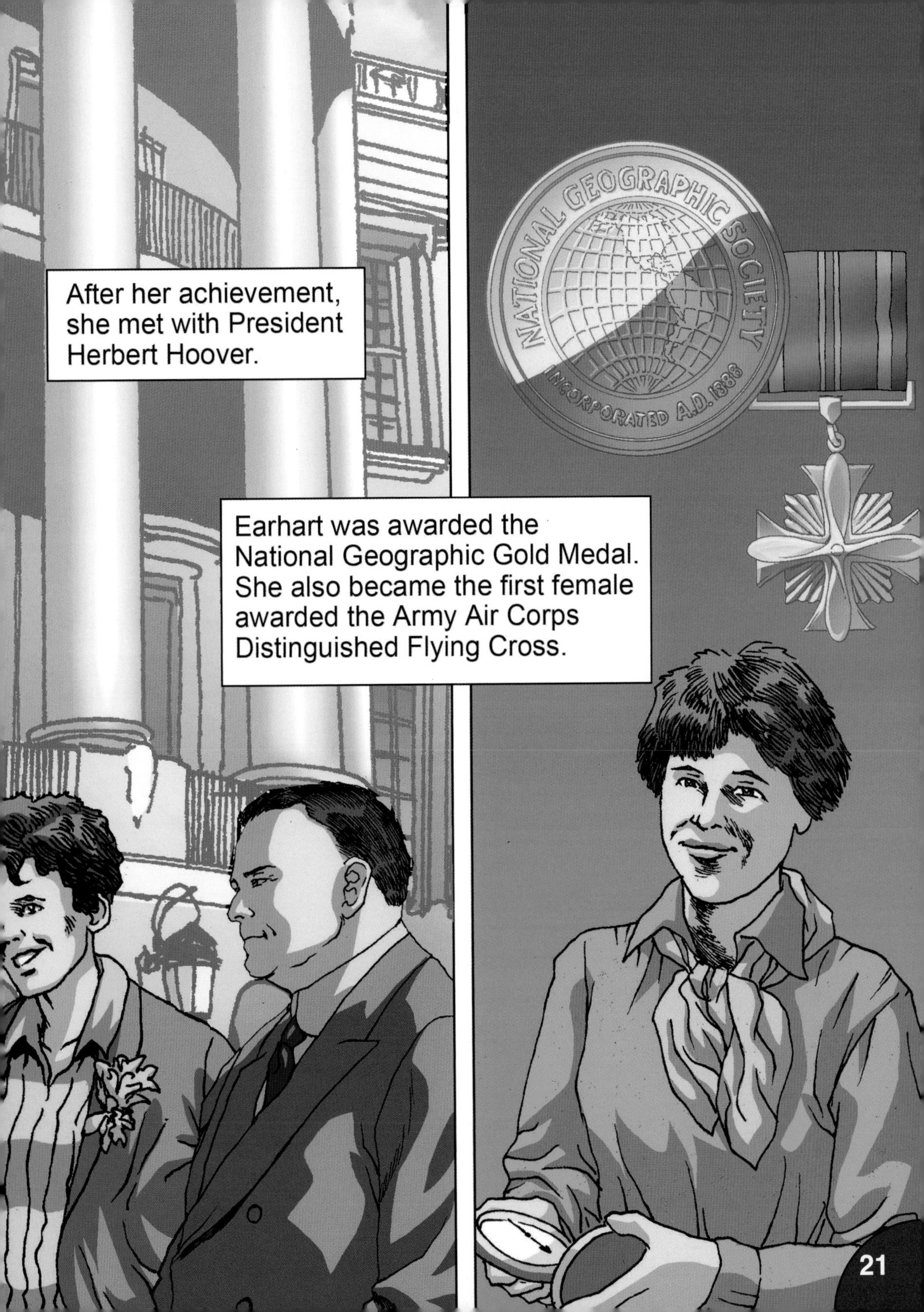
After her achievement, she met with President Herbert Hoover.
NATIONAL GEOGRAPHIC SOCIETY
INCORPORATED A.D. 1888
Earhart was awarded the National Geographic Gold Medal. She also became the first female awarded the Army Air Corps Distinguished Flying Cross.

Chapter 5 More Records

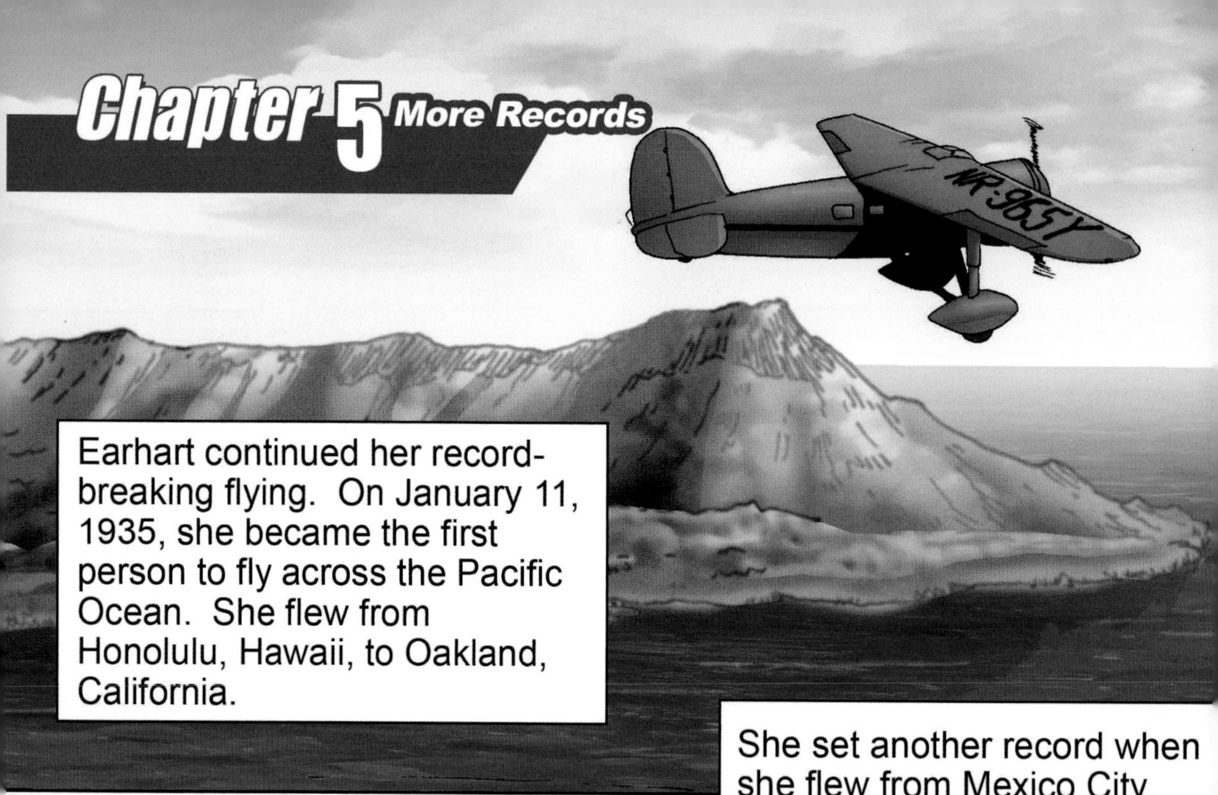
Earhart continued her record-breaking flying. On January 11, 1935, she became the first person to fly across the Pacific Ocean. She flew from Honolulu, Hawaii, to Oakland, California.
NR-965Y

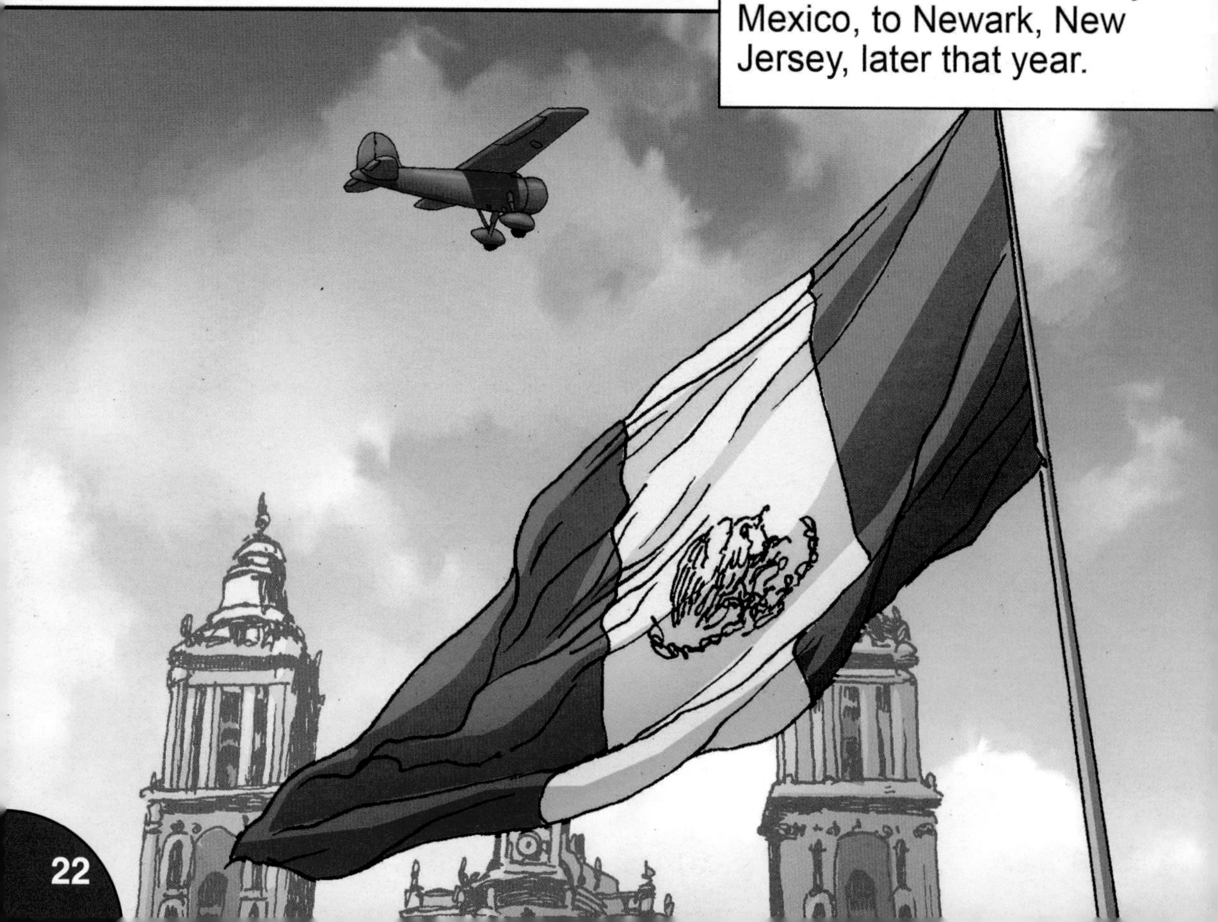
She set another record when she flew from Mexico City, Mexico, to Newark, New Jersey, later that year.

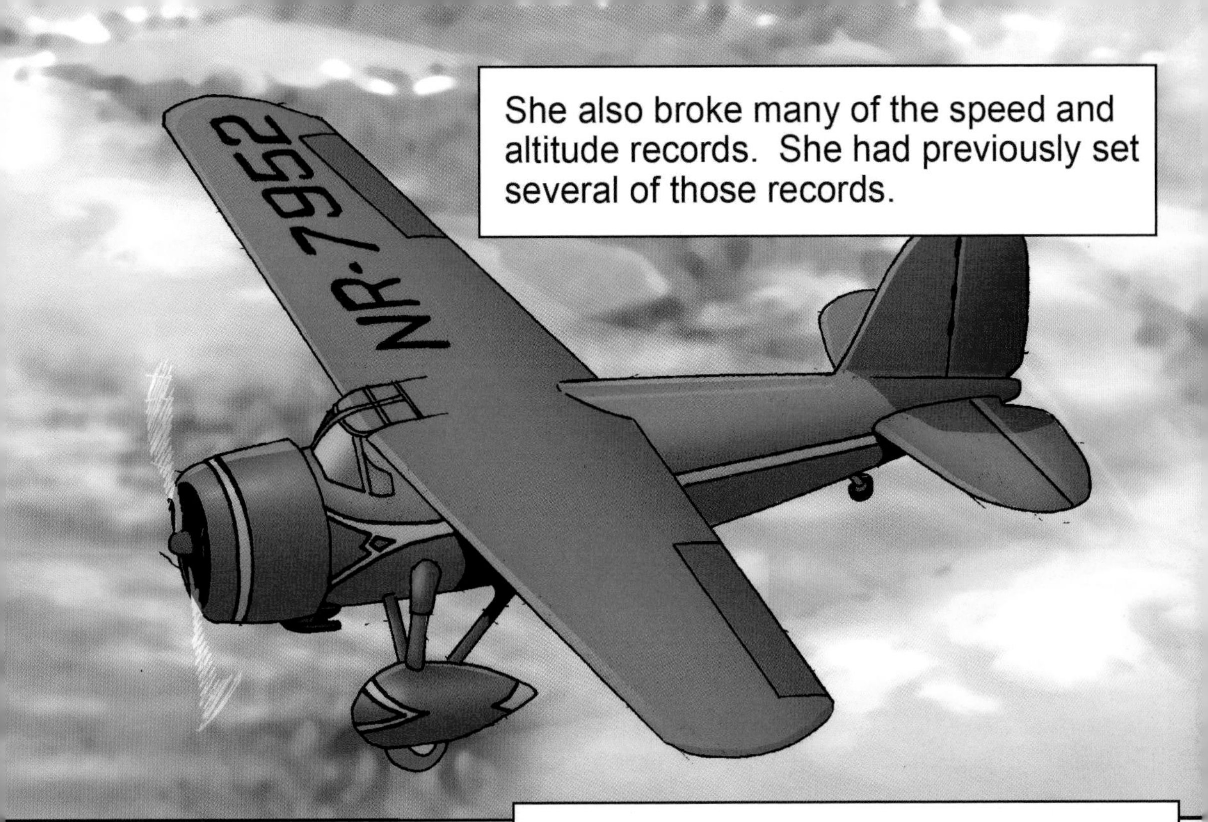
She also broke many of the speed and altitude records. She had previously set several of those records.
NR-7952

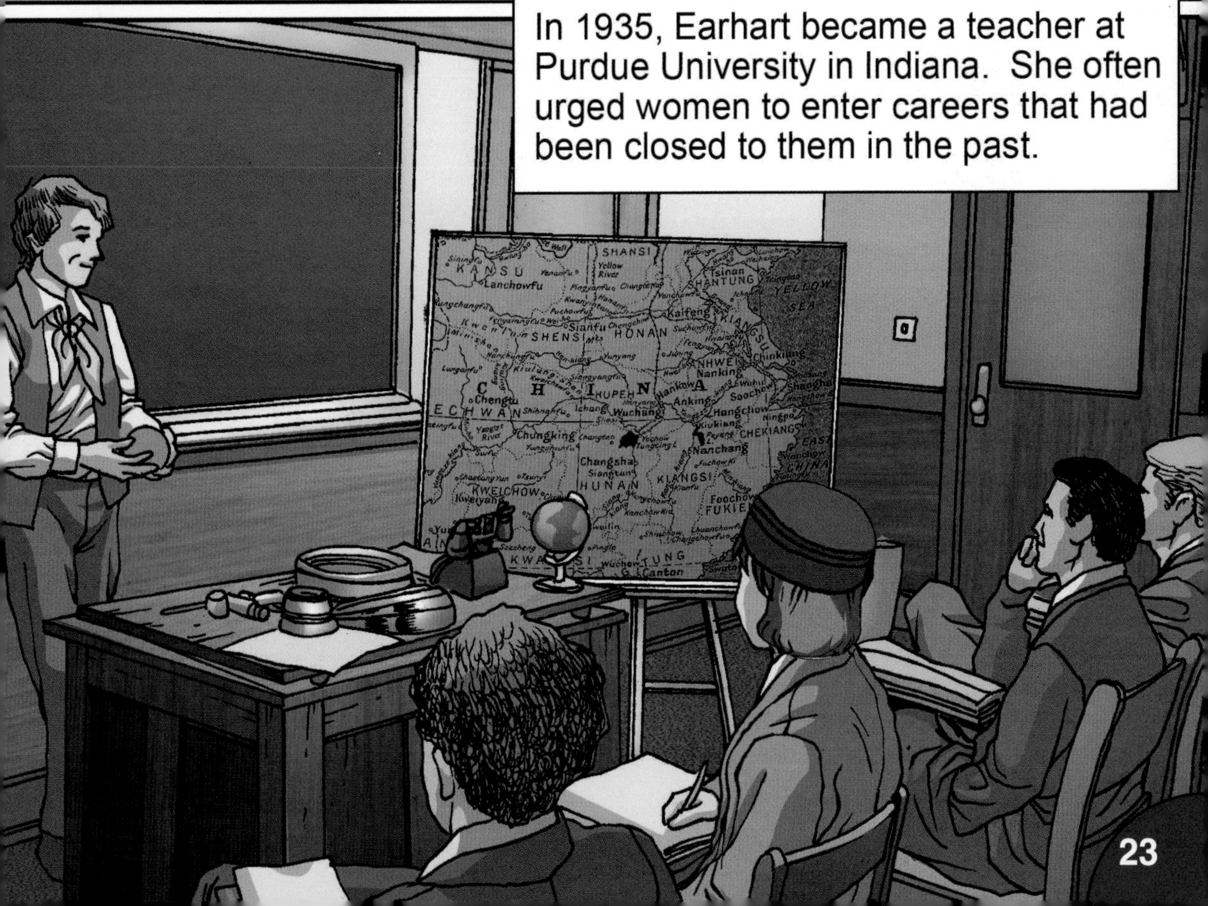
In 1935, Earhart became a teacher at Purdue University in Indiana. She often urged women to enter careers that had been closed to them in the past.

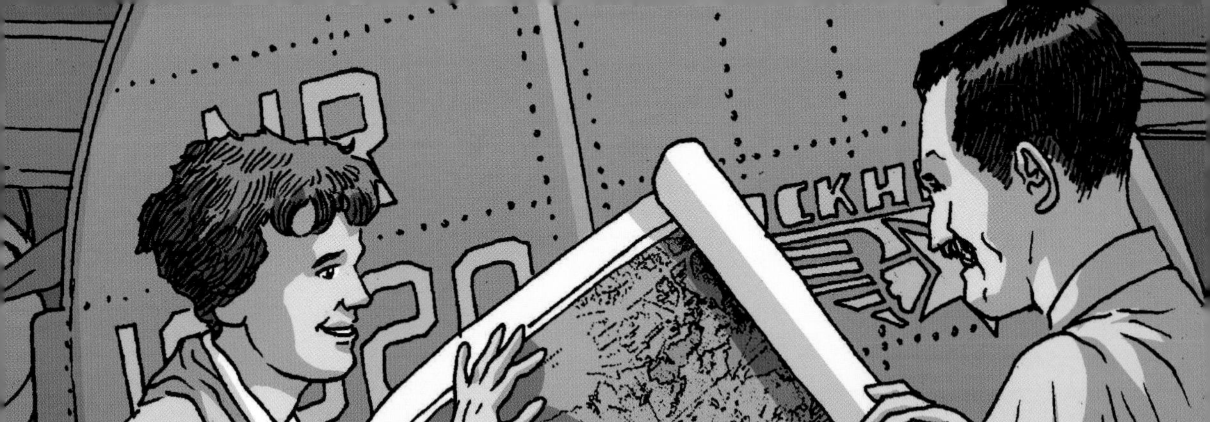
In July 1936, Earhart started planning a flight around the world. She was almost 40 years old and was ready for another challenge. The trip she planned would cover 29,000 miles.

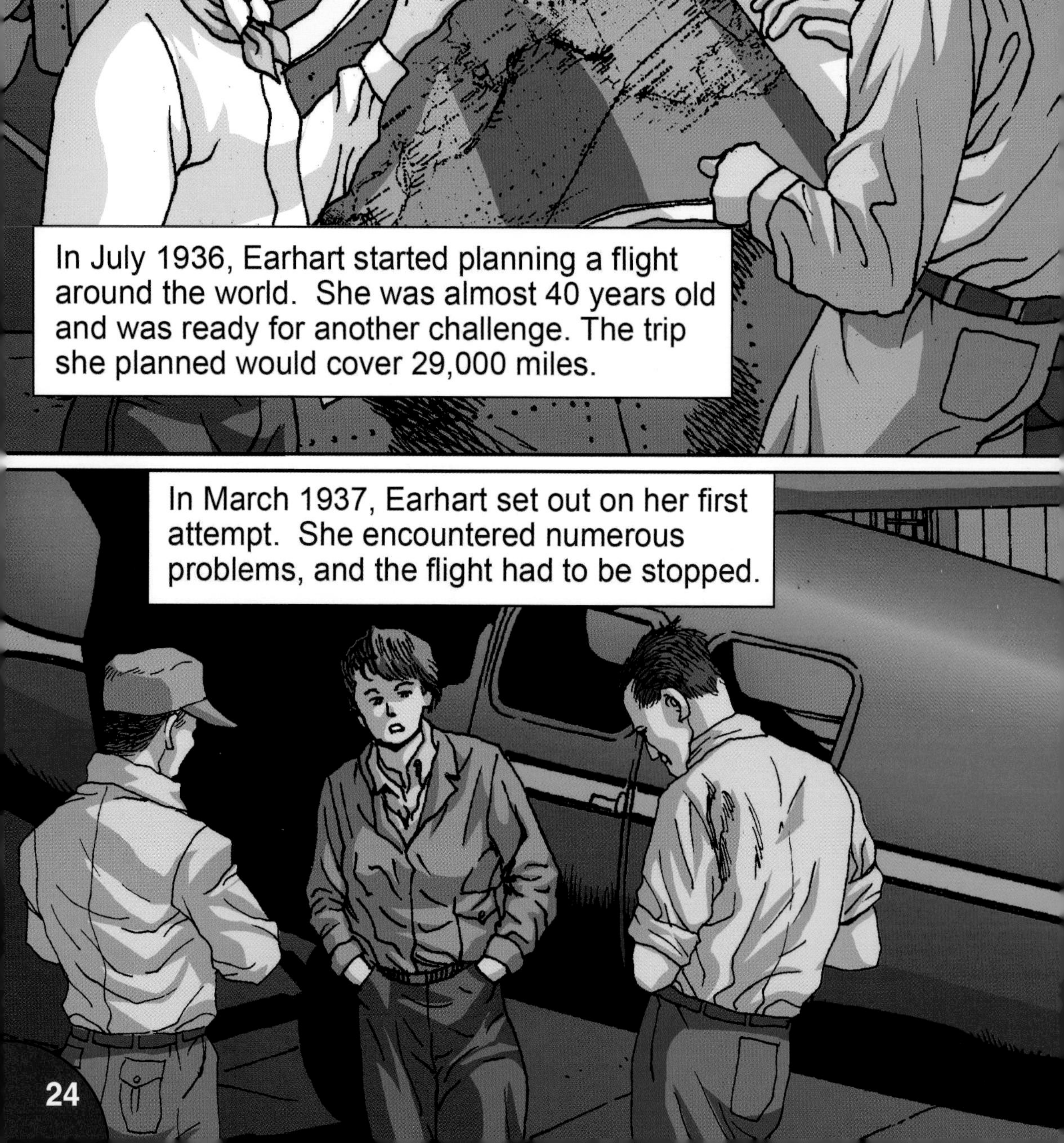
In March 1937, Earhart set out on her first attempt. She encountered numerous problems, and the flight had to be stopped.

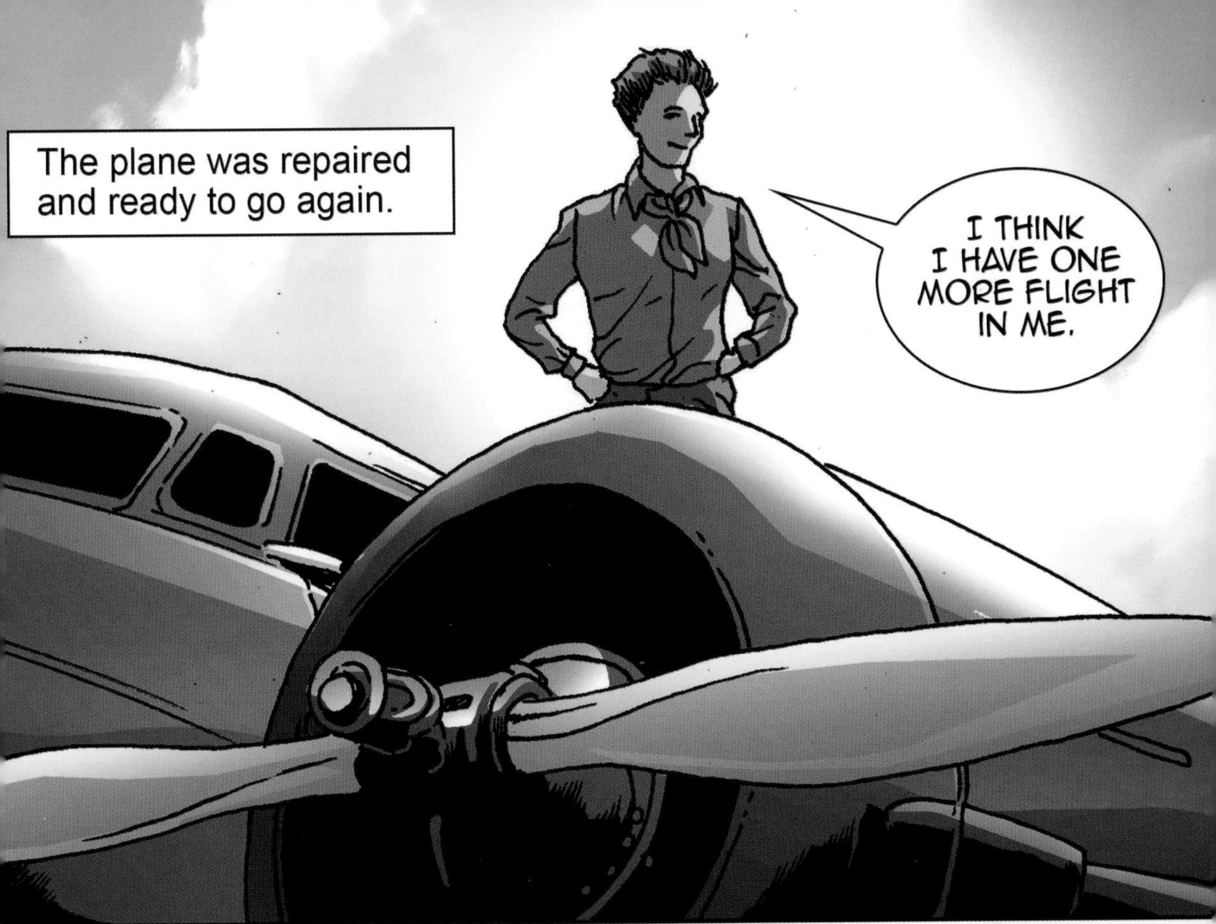
The plane was repaired and ready to go again.
I THINK I HAVE ONE MORE FLIGHT IN ME.

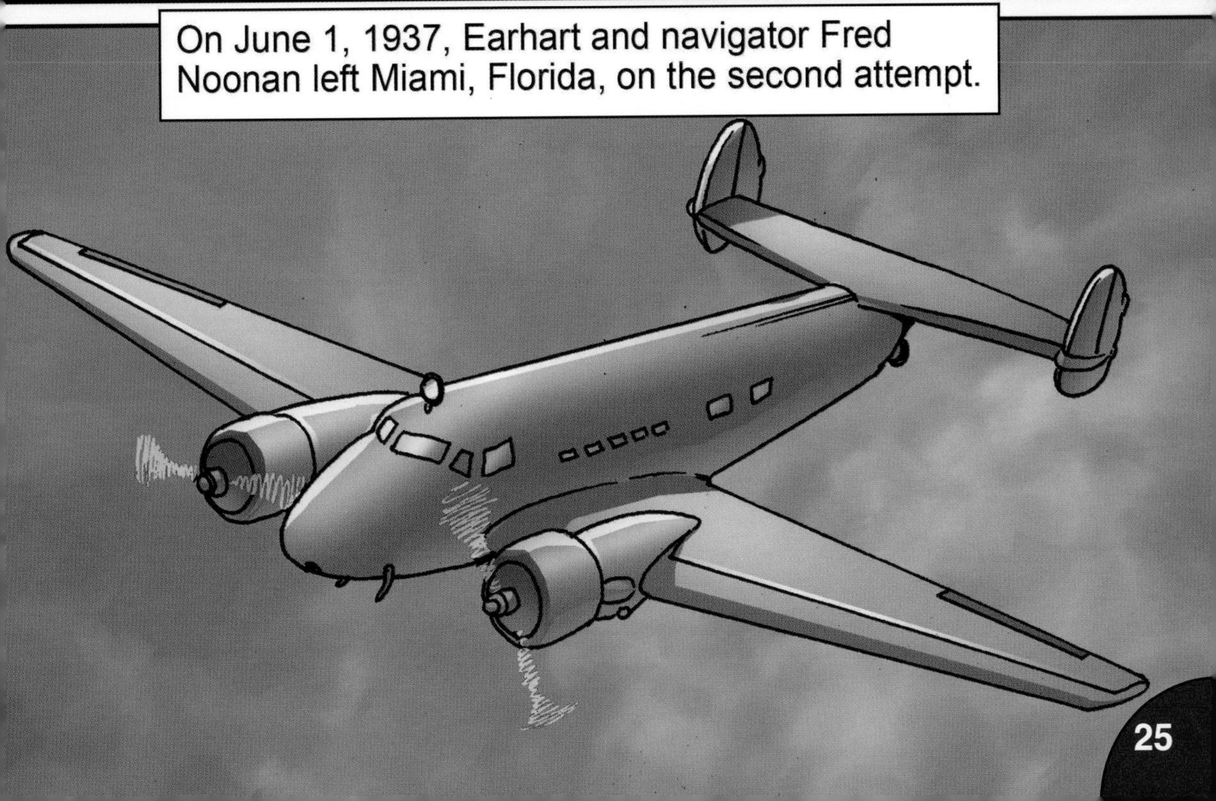
On June 1, 1937, Earhart and navigator Fred Noonan left Miami, Florida, on the second attempt.

Chapter 6 Lost at Sea

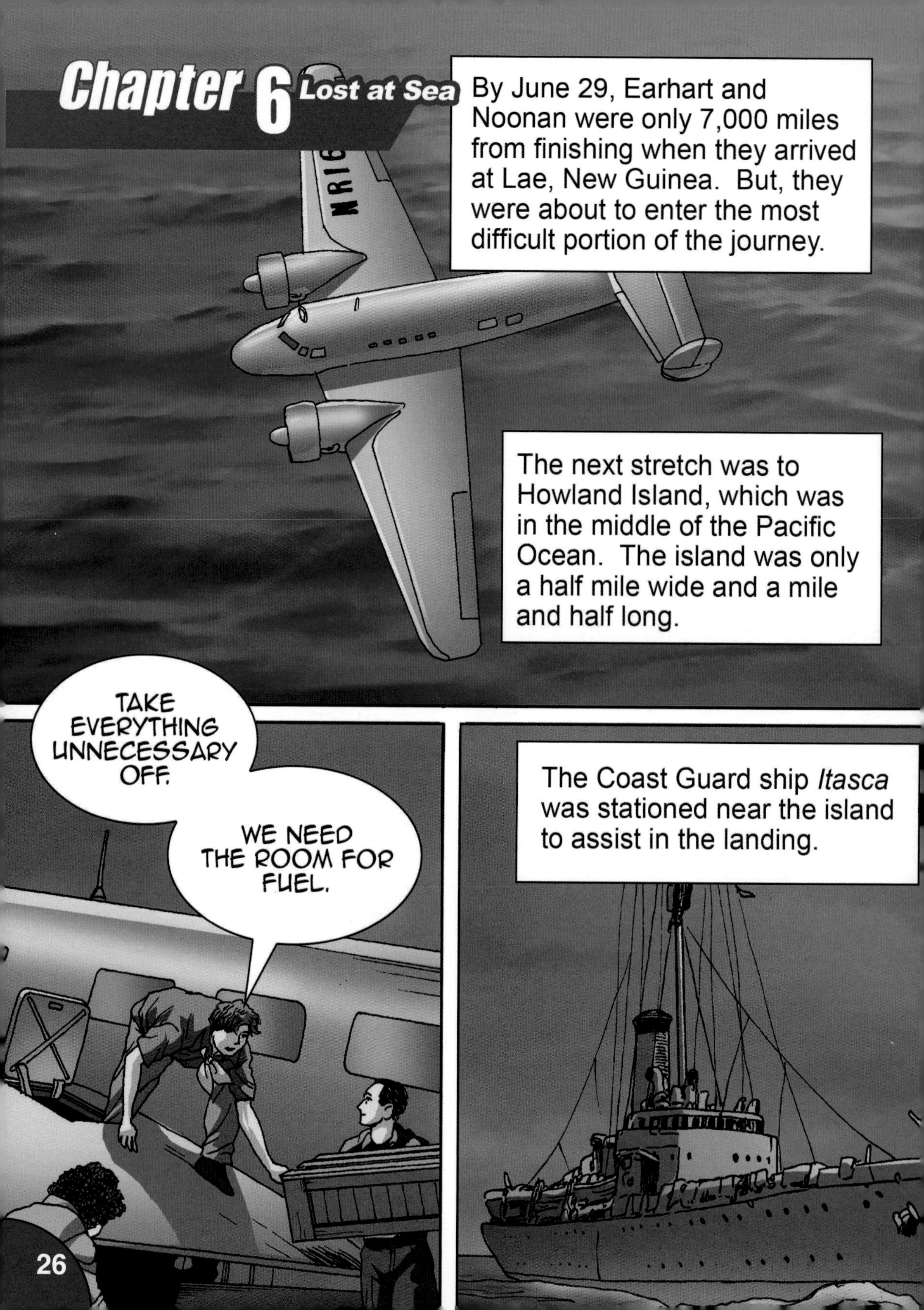
By June 29, Earhart and Noonan were only 7,000 miles from finishing when they arrived at Lae, New Guinea. But, they were about to enter the most difficult portion of the journey.
NR16
The next stretch was to Howland Island, which was in the middle of the Pacific Ocean. The island was only a half mile wide and a mile and half long.
TAKE EVERYTHING UNNECESSARY OFF.
WE NEED THE ROOM FOR FUEL.
The Coast Guard ship *Itasca* was stationed near the island to assist in the landing.

On July 2, 1937, the plane took off with good weather reports. However, Earhart and Noonan soon ran into cloudy skies, which made navigation difficult.

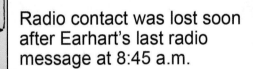

I'M GETTING STATIC. WE CAN'T SEE YOU BUT WE MUST BE NEAR. OUR FUEL IS RUNNING LOW.

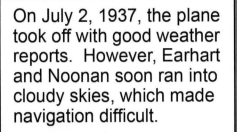

Radio contact was lost soon after Earhart's last radio message at 8:45 a.m.

COME IN... COME IN... ANYONE THERE?

The plane had sporadic radio contact with the *Itasca*.

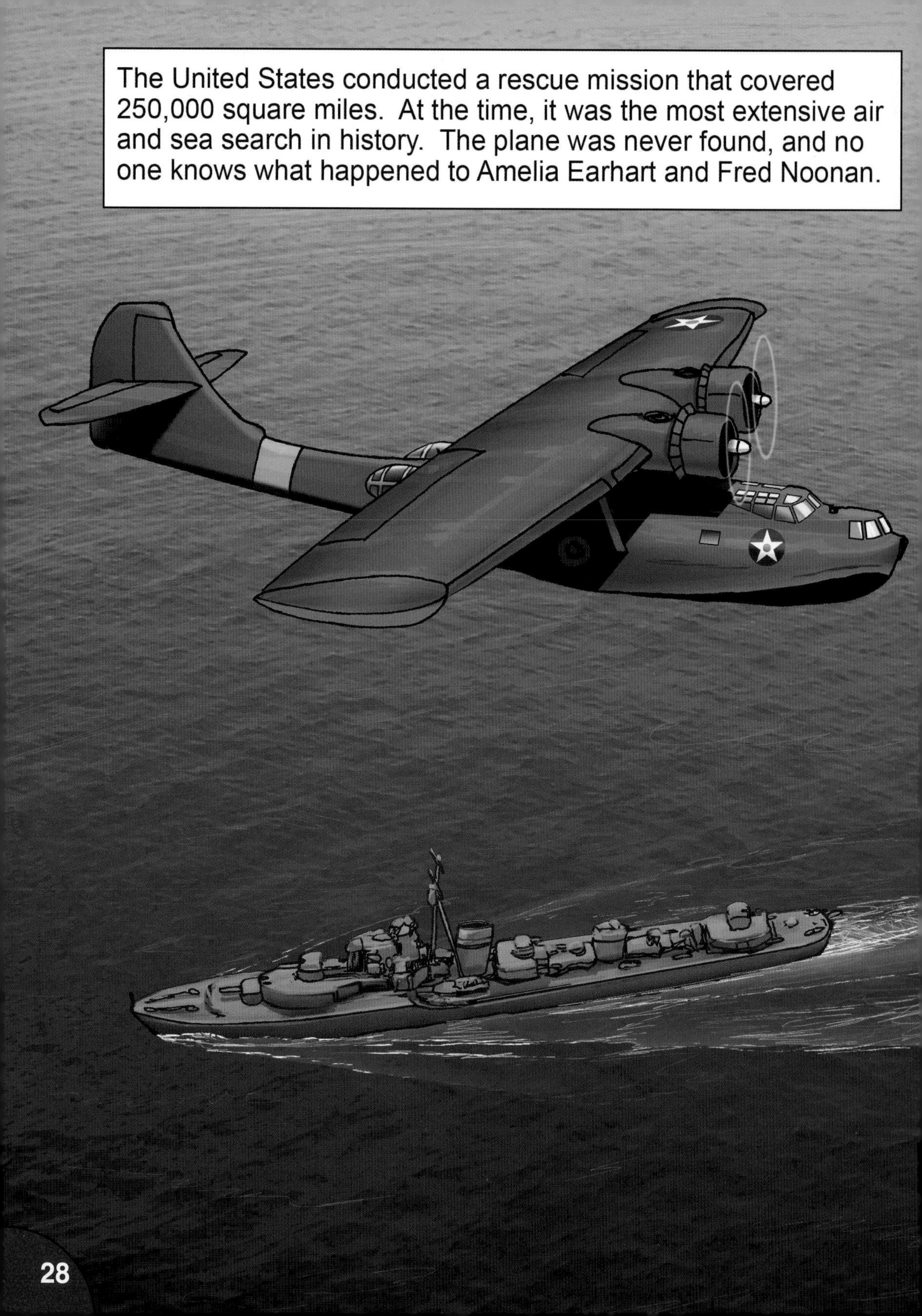
The United States conducted a rescue mission that covered 250,000 square miles. At the time, it was the most extensive air and sea search in history. The plane was never found, and no one knows what happened to Amelia Earhart and Fred Noonan.

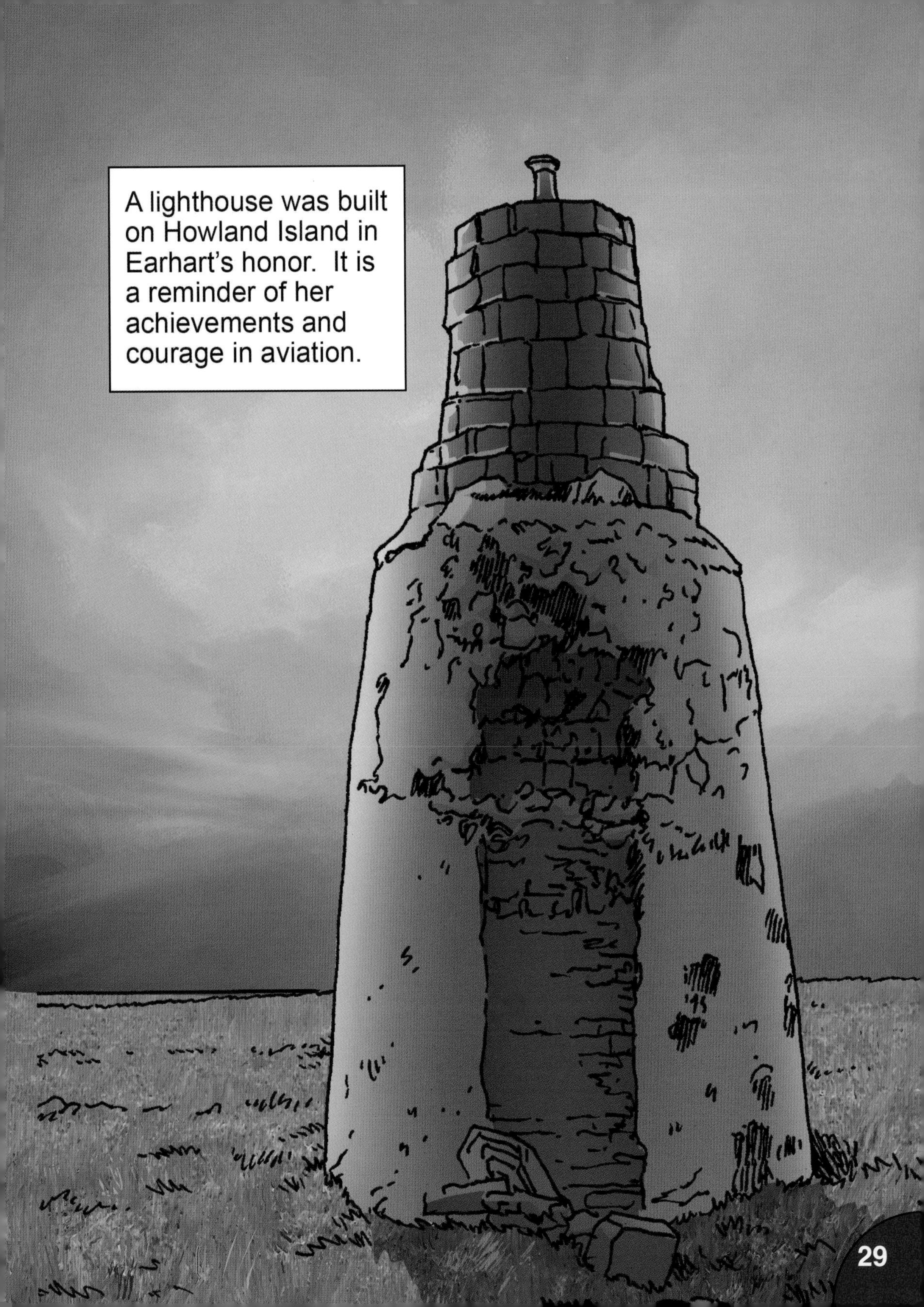
A lighthouse was built on Howland Island in Earhart's honor. It is a reminder of her achievements and courage in aviation.

Further Reading

Devillier, Christy. *Amelia Earhart.* First Biographies. Edina: ABDO Publishing Company, 2001.

Earhart, Amelia. *The Fun of It.* Chicago: Academy Chicago Publishers, 2005.

Micklos, John. *Unsolved: What Really Happened to Amelia Earhart?* New Jersey: Enslow Publishers, 2006.

Wheeler, Jill C. *Amelia Earhart.* Breaking Barriers. Edina: ABDO Publishing Company, 2002.

Glossary

aviation - the operation and navigation of aircraft. A person that operates an aircraft is called an aviator.

derby - a race or a contest open to a specified category of contestants.

gig - a booking for a job to be done in public.

nickname - a descriptive name given to a person by friends, family, or the media.

solo - something undertaken or done alone.

spokesperson - a person who is a representative of a product in order to encourage others to purchase that item. Often a spokesperson is a celebrity or a recognizable public figure.

sporadic - happening occasionally or at random times.

tomboy - a girl who behaves or does things that is considered to be boyish.

World War I - from 1914 to 1918, fought in Europe. Great Britain, France, Russia, the United States, and their allies were on one side. Germany, Austria-Hungary, and their allies were on the other side.

Web Sites

To learn more about Amelia Earhart, visit ABDO Publishing Company on the World Wide Web at www.abdopublishing.com. Web sites about Earhart are featured on our Book Links page. These links are routinely monitored and updated to provide the most current information available.

Index

A
Atlantic Ocean 13, 14, 19, 20
awards 21

C
Canary 11, 12
childhood 6, 7, 8
Coolidge, Calvin 16

E
education 9, 10, 11

F
family 6, 8, 9, 10
Friendship 15, 16

G
Gordon, Louis 15

H
Hawks, Frank 10
Hoover, Herbert 21
Howland Island 26, 29

I
Itasca 26, 27

L
Lindbergh, Charles 13, 17

N
Noonan, Fred 25, 26, 27, 28

P
Pacific Ocean 22, 26
Putnam, George 15, 18, 19

R
Railey, Hilton H. 14
records 12, 20, 22, 23

S
Snook, Neta 11
Stultz, Wilmer 15

W
Women's Air Derby 17
World War I 9